Grace Keeps You Going

Spiritual Wisdom from Cancer Survivors

Grace Keeps You Going

Spiritual Wisdom from Cancer Survivors

Mac N. and Anne Shaw Turnage

Westminster John Knox Press
LOUISVILLE • LONDON

Scripture quotations from the New Revised Standard Version of the Bible are copyright ©1989 by the Division of Christian Education of the National Council of the Churches of Christ in the U.S.A. and are used by permission.

The stories in this book come from the memory of real people, survivors of cancer, their insights, reflections and their prayers. However, as the product of memory, the authors and publishers do not claim historical accuracy. In fact, each personality or event or quotation is a composite. For instance, one story may contain elements from several different survivors. Names and locations have been changed, and every effort has been made to contact individuals for authorization to use their observations and experiences. If corrections are necessary, they will be made in subsequent printings.

Book design by Sharon Adams
Cover design by Pam Poll Graphic Design

First edition
Published by Westminster John Knox Press
Louisville, Kentucky

This book is printed on acid-free paper that meets the American National Standards Institute Z39.48 standard. ♾

PRINTED IN THE UNITED STATES OF AMERICA

01 02 03 04 05 06 07 08 09 10–10 9 8 7 6 5 4 3 2 1

Cataloging-in-Publication Data is on file at the Library of Congress, Washington, D.C.

ISBN 0-664-22567-5

Dedicated to
OUR FAMILY,
who have shared our lives—
the fears and frustrations,
joys and pains,
uncertainties and victories—
during the years
since our cancer diagnosis in 1973
and to
the throng of friends and cancer survivors
who have honored us by becoming
OUR EXTENDED FAMILY,
especially
the CanCare staff, board members and volunteers,
and the Friends of CanCare,
as well as
oncologists and other partners on
OUR HEALING TEAM

Contents

Foreword

The Turnages came into my life while I was recovering from surgery for thyroid cancer. Lying in a hospital bed, I was hurting as much emotionally as physically. Instead of a brief operation for a simple problem, I had spent six hours in surgery and was wrung out from the devastating news that I had entered the world of cancer. My mind was a jumble of questions. Would I live to see my young son Tommy grow up? What would my husband do without me? Was I going to die?

It was the summer of 1990. Mac Turnage, one of the pastors of our church, visited us immediately after my operation. I was unable to talk, so he had a quiet, comforting conversation with my mother. He told us about CanCare, a new faith-based cancer ministry, and offered to have his wife Anne, the director, contact us.

In the days that followed, Anne Turnage stopped in several times, first at the hospital and later in our home. Better than a therapist, she slowly repaired my shattered morale. Feeling helpless was new to me, but Anne's strength quickly became my strength. Seventeen years earlier, she had been where I was, a frightened young mother with a young family. Her emergency surgery revealed advanced colon cancer with metastasis to the liver. Our friendship grew through my period of recovery.

I was so grateful for Anne's help in my down period that I offered to help further her cause. First, I went through the training program for volunteers, the ones who make up the backbone of CanCare's service. My first task was writing a grant proposal to the Junior League for money to hire a full-time associate. Since we lost our family medical insurance because of my cancer, I needed to find work. I applied for the grant and the job. Luckily, I got both.

As we worked together, I learned that Anne had blended her personal experience as a cancer survivor with her professional endeavors in Christian education. I also found out that in their crisis, she and Mac had promised each other that if she survived the first year of the disease, they would pour their energies into writing a book to encourage other cancer patients to embrace hope. The result, titled *More Than You Dare to Ask*, details Anne and Mac's courageous stand.

But that was not all. She went on to establish in Richmond, Virginia, a support service to give hope to cancer survivors. Their root belief was that no one should ever have to go through the devastating experience of cancer alone. In 1980, the Turnages moved to Charlotte, North Carolina. There Anne launched another free support service for cancer survivors, recruiting men and women with cancer experience and training them to reach out in friendship, one on one, to people just entering the scary world of cancer. The Turnages kept refining their concept over the next several years as the organization grew to meet the expanding needs of their new community.

Anne's reputation for her cancer support work had preceded her when the Turnages moved to Houston in 1989. A church grant enabled her to create a volunteer cancer support network to help Houstonians weather the storm of cancer.

Our paths merged when I discovered that I had thyroid cancer. With Anne's organizational talents and ability to work with people along with my marketing and business experience, we made a great team. With the help of a dynamic board of directors, the early volunteers helped us recruit others and they helped interpret the ministry to congregations and to the medical world. An auxiliary group, Friends of CanCare, took over public relations, fund-raising, and morale building. Many of these cared about the cause but had not experienced cancer themselves. We spent intense efforts building a sense of community among the volunteers, so that they gave support to one another as well as to the persons they were looking after individually. The magic of wholesome concern in CanCare was like electricity.

The success of CanCare of Houston's first ten years stemmed in large degree from Anne Turnage's contagious enthusiasm, her incredible energy, her executive drive, and her strong faith in God. In rallying support for her cause during those early days, she spent as much time in corporate boardrooms as she did in the more familiar surroundings of religion and education.

In this book, the Turnages tell scores of brief stories from the lives of cancer survivors, stories they have shared with others over the years. Some are ironic, some funny, some sad. They are as varied as life itself, filled with ups and downs, and told with insight and compassion that only people who have lived in the cancer world themselves could provide.

Nancy N. Tucker

Introduction

Cancer Survivors

The Things They Say

"Living with cancer is like running a race with no end."

"My cancer made me feel like the heroine in a melodrama. I was the damsel in distress tied to the railroad track. A freight train was bearing down on me, but I was rescued in the nick of time."

"My life didn't end. My body was damaged. My brains were assaulted. My emotions got jangled. My spirit was bruised. But I'm still alive!"

"My cancer experience has been like working a giant jigsaw puzzle, with pieces missing and with no idea what the picture is going to look like."

The Lives They Live

Alma is a professional counselor, an eighteen-year survivor of lung cancer. She plays tennis with her husband, enjoys her grandchildren, and has walked the twenty-six-mile course in the city's annual marathon. She spends time and energy in training volunteers. She is in constant touch with other survivors and develops programs that help people with cancer.

Fletcher, a prominent administrator in his school system, blames cancer of the mouth and tongue for his divorce. He has appeared on television and in other public scenes as a spokesperson for cancer survivors.

Maxine is a fifteen-year survivor of ovarian cancer with two later recurrences. During these years, she lost her husband to cancer. Recently, she married again and is employed as the coordinator of volunteers in CanCare, a service that offers friendship and encouragement to cancer survivors and their families.

Ira works for his family business, in both accounting and human relations. Ten years ago, he was diagnosed with a rare and deadly form of brain cancer (gleeoblastoma). He works out at the gym regularly, befriends other young persons with brain cancer, and is regarded as an eligible young bachelor on the social scene.

Libby has enjoyed a number of national conferences for cancer survivors, including several for her ethnic group. A nurse, she owns and operates a care home for the elderly and handicapped. Her health history includes diabetes, breast cancer with several recurrences, and two toe amputations.

These and other little known heroes and heroines are the cancer survivors who fill the pages of this book. Their stories portray the dramatic struggles and victories of people quietly dealing with their disease and living well.

The Prayers They Offer

Through tears and laughter, these heroes and heroines have found themselves praying spontaneously, almost automatically. Many of these prayers do not take formal or pious shape. Often they are simple cries for help, whimpers of thanks. Occasionally they fit into words. Some of them probe for meanings and mine great depths.

Regardless of their religious and ethnic backgrounds, in spite of or because of their faith traditions—or with no previous piety—many find lively contact with God. They pray insistently for healing and strength, and they continue this direct contact, in whatever terms they choose to address the Almighty.

The Values They Claim

We cancer survivors find that we get encouragement and nurture by telling our stories and hearing the stories of others who've been through it.

We've found mysterious bonds with other survivors, bonds that set up patterns of exchange, so we share or borrow, give or get what we need—hope, joy, peace, comfort, faith, spiritual insights.

We discover depths of meaning, profound convictions that propel us forward, making us willing to take risks and to build dreams.

We affirm the necessity of hope, pulling us forward and enabling us to set goals, to sort our priorities, to build new lifestyles, to shape rich life, and to meet the future's uncertainty with confidence.

We know, despite the permanent threat hanging over us, that God has given us a second chance, calling us to express our thanks by living fully each day.

Chapter 1

Meeting the Challenge

"I'm a cancer survivor, since I didn't drop dead when I was told I have cancer."

"Can you believe that I was relieved when they told me I had cancer? I was glad the tests were over, the uncertainty was lifted, and the medical world could help me deal with my problem. I couldn't win the war if the enemy is permanent uncertainty."

Hattie's Psychic Thud

Jennie and her daughter Clea were waiting to have mammograms. Jennie remembered the day, thirty years earlier, when her mother, Hattie, found that she had cancer. A total surprise, discovered during a routine physical exam, it was a disruption in Hattie's busy life.

Jennie said, "I think it was her first visit to a doctor after my younger brother was born. I've read her diary from those days, about her illness."

Clea asked, "Did she go to pieces? In that day, it must have been awful."

"She didn't panic, as I recall. Of course, she also told me about it. She'd noticed a place on the surface of her skin. It was a few years before you were born. She was in her late forties. Later, she worried that you and I might someday have to deal with this awful disease. We hadn't heard of any cancer in the family before."

"Well," said Clea, "she must have been horrified. I expect to be, if I ever get word that I have cancer. I hate this mammogram, because it forces me to think about the danger."

"Your grandmother didn't have much time to think. One afternoon, she went for a checkup in the doctor's office. The next morning she was in the hospital for surgery. She wrote in her diary about the THUD that hit her psyche."

Both sat in solemn thought for a moment. Watching her daughter carefully, Jennie invited, "You seem to have something to say."

After a sigh, Clea muttered, "This conversation isn't the best preparation for a mammogram. Let's talk about something else for a few minutes, before our names are called. When they do call for us, I want you to go in first for the ceremonial smashing of the female breast."

"Clea, what would we do without your sense of humor? Say what you will, I'm glad these machines improve our chances of early detection and better treatment. But can anything ever prevent that THUD? By the way, there's a note scribbled in the margin of that diary, an entry written years later. It says,'I recovered from the operation, but I never recovered from that THUD.'"

Rosalie's Relief

By telephone, when she made the appointment, Rosalie had introduced herself as a strong person, an athlete and sports enthusiast. Dr. Spann, the surgeon, noticed when he met her that she matched her description, short and sturdy and in good health. But he was not prepared for this new patient.

She explained, "I found the lump and was sure it was malignant, even before they did the tests and gave me the results." While Dr. Spann was examining her, she announced that both breasts were to be removed.

Startled, Dr. Spann assured her, "That won't be necessary!"

She insisted, "Doctor, these huge boobs have been a problem for me since I was a young girl. I'm glad to get rid of them. My husband agrees."

The surgeon protested, "But only your left breast is diseased. You don't need such extensive surgery. Just calm down. Be glad that you don't need drastic measures."

"I am calm. And I'll be glad to get rid of both. I don't need to be a single-breasted female. These organs served their purpose. The one that's not diseased is useless tissue as far as we're concerned. It's another area subject to attack, a large area. Hell, doctor, if you don't take them both off, I won't be able to walk straight."

After other arguments and further collaboration, she had a bilateral mastectomy and was recovering well. During her hospitalization, Rosalie received a telephone call from a Reach to Recovery volunteer. She explained that she had "similar surgery several years ago. In this American Cancer Society program, we visitors have the doctor's approval and I want to meet you." She explained, "I can demonstrate some exercises and give you a temporary prosthesis, so I need to know your bra size."

Rosalie quickly responded, "That's fine, dear. I'll be glad for a visit, and I'm sure you and the exercises will help. I'm an athlete. I play golf and tennis, and I'm eager to get on with my life. But I want the smallest prosthesis you have—cup size A minus, or whatever you call it."

"Oh, no," was the reply. "The smallest size is no bigger than an enlarged pimple. You don't want that."

"That's exactly what I want. I want to be more like Twiggy and less like Dolly. I'm relieved to be rid of those two large breasts. They were a burden. I lost twenty-eight pounds in the operation. And besides, my husband has promised me a complete wardrobe for my new figure. When can you visit, dear?"

Help, God—I'm Your Needy Child

I don't know how to deal with
  the mood-swings whirling me around,
    slinging me up and down,
      back and forth,
  the questions with no answers,
  the uncertainties I can't avoid,
  the ghost of recurrence haunting me,
  the threat of death forcing me to face my limits,
  the losses I've sustained.
I don't like my lack of control
  over my days,
  over my nights,
  over my destiny.
I don't expect to get all the problems solved
  or all the questions answered,
but I do want to use good judgment,
  to maintain basic dignity,
  to make sound decisions,
  to choose constructive steps to take,
  to develop realistic plans,
  to march in the victory parade.
Please!

Promises—Not Alone

GOD, YOU promised
that I would never
be alone,
that YOU
are always
here.

I believe
YOUR promises.

But I am lonely.

And YOU are here.
Please show up,
or send someone!

Together—Creator and Creatures

GOD, YOU are the one who knits us together.
Now, with my people, I affirm
    that all caring, however clumsy, is helping,
    that not-leaving instills strength,
    that symbolic and concrete acts have healing effects.
We don't like the shape life has taken, but
    we are committed to our life together—
    with all the bumps and jolts,
    the dark valleys and the bright hillsides,
    the disasters and troubles,
    the delights and pleasures.

Weave our pattern so that our companionship
    takes in this ailment
    without letting it become a barrier between us,
so that together we find times and places
    for laughter as well as tears,
    for silence as well as conversations,
    for free decisions as well as necessary arrangements,
    for creative plans as well as emergency measures.
Help us complete the fabric.

Leslie's Search

Leslie was apprehensive that her sorority sisters wanted her to help them learn about their classmate's cancer situation. Suzy, the sister with Hodgkin's disease, had been forced to drop out of school.

One of the sisters said, "Leslie, you're headed for med school. Why don't you investigate for all of us, find out what we need to know."

Leslie gathered information about Hodgkin's disease and learned that it is mainly a disease of young people. She was encouraged that it is curable. The treatments can be rough, and they can last for weeks or even months.

Later Leslie asked chaplains, "When patients find out that they have cancer, how do they respond? What do they say and think and feel?" From these interviews, she recorded quotes: "In my wildest dreams, I never believed that I could have cancer." "There are so many really bad people—why did I get cancer? At least, I try to live a good life." "Where's God? Does God know or care what's happening to me?" "I've gone to Sunday school and church all my life. My husband and I are bringing up our children that way. We read the Bible every day. Now, God let this happen to me." "What did I do to cause this?"

One chaplain insisted that Leslie use the term "cancer survivor" rather than "cancer victim" or "cancer patient."

Then Leslie decided, "I need to talk with someone who's been through the cancer experience, or someone who's dealing with it at the moment. Then I should be able to tell the other girls what I've learned. Maybe we'll come up with some practical ways to help Suzy and her family. And maybe I'll get into oncology some day. I see it as a field for a caring person."

Camille's Camp Adventure

Helen was glad to hear that her daughter Camille had a great time at the summer camp for children with cancer. She could hear the girl's enthusiasm, "We found out why it's called 'CAmp CARE.' CA stands for Cancer, and CARE means 'Cancer Ain't Really the End.'"

Helen recalled, "The child had been through so much. Cancer is awful! And having her leg amputated made it so much more serious. At first, I said she couldn't go to camp. I had a hard time agreeing to be away from her for a week. The camp director and Camille's favorite nurse warned me about being overprotective, so I had to give in."

On her return, Camille bragged to Helen, "I was named Queen for the Day because everyone was so proud of me. The nurses and the counselors chose me because I haven't been in the hospital for the last two years."

Later in the summer, she told her mother, "When I go back to school this year, I'll have something to tell about and write about. The teacher always makes us tell what we did in the summer. I'll be able to talk about camp and being Queen for the Day instead of having to tell about cancer treatments and the hospital."

"Honey, we both can celebrate your good summer. And your good health!"

David's Diagnosis

For fourteen-year-old David, the diagnosis was leukemia. It came after weeks of "feeling rotten"—weakness and headaches and stressful tests. He could hardly work up energy to respond to the news. He was miserable. His parents were trying not to be alarmed. The specialists had been frustrated. He was losing strength daily, but none of their suspicions or studies had produced firm answers.

After the initial shock, the family reviewed the distress David was dragged through and the fears they were fighting. His mother chattered as though reciting a memorized story. "He's usually so energetic and such a good athlete, involved in all the sports. Of course, his favorite is football. He was quarterback on the junior high team, and he was hoping to make the varsity team in his sophomore year. He was eager to move up. He's been so sick that he hasn't even mentioned his prospects for next fall. And he's missing the whole baseball season. He did get fired up when some of the Braves team visited him and other children in the hospital last week. When David's not excited about professional sports figures, this kid is sick!"

Once the label was placed on his illness, the medical experts rallied their resources to get the disease under control. They explained that chemotherapy could be effective in a matter of weeks and that a complete cure could be expected. At that point, David was so sick he appeared uninterested. Asked if he was ready to take the necessary treatment, he solemnly nodded his assent.

"You asked how we are feeling?" his mother Nicole answered a neighbor. "All four of us feel that we've been run over by a truck. David's so weak. It's hard to know what his feelings are. The other three of us talked last night at home, after we got the word. We're relieved to know that something can be done. We don't have to fight uncertainty any longer.

"But it's a killer disease we're dealing with. We're glad the doctors are confident about the treatments. They promise successful recovery, but we're holding our breath too. He's still in danger and we're still terrified.

"We dread the treatments. They'll be hard on him. He's tough, and we're all trying to be brave. At the same time, we're scared out of our wits, tied up in knots. All of us are bundles of jangled emotions. But we're ready to fight, and we need help. Thanks for asking."

A Plea for New Perspectives

YOU see everything, GOD.
I need help in getting new perspectives.

Sometimes I think they are all staring at me,
    knowing that I carry "the Big C,"
    thinking that I have to be treated in strange ways,
    wondering how to talk with me or to me,
    worrying about whether they will get it,

but they don't say anything aloud,
at least not to me.

At other times, they don't seem to notice me,
    forgetting that I have "the Big C,"
    treating me as if I were normal,
    chattering about senseless trivia,
    acting as though everyone will be healthy
    always,
    but I don't dare mention my worries aloud, not
    to them.

Maybe I'm preoccupied.
Maybe they don't know.
Maybe YOU want me to see that the world is bigger
    than my restricted views, problems, suspicions.

Help me focus my vision.

Gwen's Bandage

Several years after her "cancer scare," Gwen was describing her encounter with the disease. Her sister Erin had discovered a lump in her own breast and was afraid for her future. She asked Gwen to tell her what happened in her experience fifteen years earlier.

Gwen began, "In those days, when anyone discovered a lump in her breast, she had to sign papers authorizing the surgeon to remove the lump. And at the same time, I had to sign a statement giving permission for them to remove the whole breast if a malignancy was found. They took a portion of the tissue and examined what they called a 'frozen section.' Since then, the experts may have improved the process, but maybe not.

"My dear husband Calvin stuck with me through all the conferences. As I signed the papers, he was there, keeping my morale up. That was a big part of my support and confidence. As I went into the operation, the surgeon explained again that when I woke up and felt my breast, I would know whether I had cancer or not. If I found a large bandage, where my left breast had been, I would know that I'd had a radical mastectomy. If the breast was there with a bandage on it, I would know that the tumor was benign."

She described the moment of discovery. "As I was creeping back into consciousness, even before I opened my eyes, I was aware that Calvin was clasping my hand. I eased my right hand loose and grabbed for my left breast. There was no large bandage! The breast was still there! My own grin helped me open my eyes. And the first thing I saw was Calvin standing beside the bed with a matching smile on his face. I remember saying quietly, 'Thank You, God!' and I heard Calvin's loud 'Amen!' before I backed away, into peaceful sleep."

Erin said, "At this next meeting with my surgeon, I'll find out what procedures he expects to use. Thanks for filling me in on your history. My husband will be there too, so I'll have someone to hold my hand—and to say 'Amen!'"

JoAnn's Thank-You Letter

Dear Vera,

It's good to be home. It's a little scary too, but it's good. Thanks for your visit at the hospital and all the phone calls.

Ovarian cancer! I still can't believe it's happened to me. But I do have reminders—abdominal soreness and scars, not being able to drive. And the pain is quite real.

I must still be in shock. It seems impossible—a bad ultrasound one afternoon and less than two days later I was in the hospital for the operation.

We go back next week to meet with the oncologist, to talk about treatment. Thank goodness there's something more to be done. All I could think of was how can I get everything done that I need to do, so Michael will be all right without me. The children are at such a tender age. I hope God will let me live at least until they finish high school.

The doctors all tell us that there's no one reason why I got cancer. No one else has ever had cancer in my family. I never smoked. But I keep wondering if I did something to cause this dreadful disease. I wouldn't have done this to Michael and the children for anything.

I'm trying to pray. Really, I'm begging God to help me—us—through this so that it won't leave scars on our children or wound our family life. I need someone to say words I can't put together, to tell God for me that I need hope, that I want to live as a healthy person, and that I am so scared about what's ahead.

Thanks for wanting to know what I'm going through. Please keep up your prayers for me. And let's find time to talk soon.

Love,
JoAnn

Giving and Getting Aid

These people close to me are ailing
　　because of my condition.
In their eyes I read disappointment,
　　frustration,
　　pain,
　　fear.

Cure them, please.

Protect them from damage.
Give them serenity.
Help them find ways to be helpful,
　　even though they can't "fix it."
Give them tolerance for what they can't understand.
Let them know that their presence brings me strength.

Comfort and encourage them.

Help me tell them, even though I can't say it,
   that their gestures,
   their closeness,
   their thoughtful acts,
   their physical aid,
   their joyful presence
are channels of YOUR grace
   while I'm still sick,
   while the disease dominates us,
   while all of us
     hate what we're going through.

Carolyn's Conversations

Carolyn couldn't talk about her first encounter with cancer to anyone except her physician. "I learned to deal with it privately and clinically," she said.

Later, Dr. Norman led her to talk about how lonely she had been during her ordeal. "No one ever asked about my feelings during that time. And I didn't want to burden my teenage daughters or my hardworking husband."

Dr. Norman encouraged her to sign up for training with other cancer survivors. CanCare was recruiting volunteers who were to befriend persons dealing with cancer. "It's a new program. I've also urged your friend Shannon to go. You can check it out and then decide whether to make a commitment."

Helping others appealed to Carolyn and Shannon, so they agreed to go through the training. They told their own stories and practiced their "listening skills" as others told their stories. They learned about the disease and methods of treatment.

After several months, Carolyn learned that her cancer had returned. She and her family had new patterns of communicating. She had good coaching from her physicians. She learned that she would have surgery and then follow-up chemotherapy.

She insisted that her husband Tom sit with her during her conferences with the doctors. "He was brave about it, but he was uncomfortable. At home, I gently talked about my fears and hopes, and he listened quietly. Before the operation, I talked with both daughters and their husbands. My partners in the CanCare group were eager to give moral support."

Carolyn observed, "I was stronger the second time. All of us—Tom and I and our children—are focused and together. We have a crew of friends who know what it's like to deal with cancer. It's still tough, but I'm not flying solo now."

Donna's Delightful Day

Over more than twenty years, Donna had multiple encounters with cancer. She welcomed invitations to speak about her experiences.

At a conference for oncology nurses, she was on a panel of experienced, healthy patients. The leader explained, "Nurses in the hospital see patients in trauma, soon after diagnosis, during treatments, or when they're dying. The survivors on this panel have different perspectives."

Each panel member sketched a story of illness, treatment, and recovery. "My disease is arrested," one said, "but there's no cure yet for my brand of cancer." Another had experienced three incidents, each a different disease but all cancer.

Then a young nurse asked Donna, "How can you be so hopeful when you've had trouble over so many years? Were you always enthusiastic about life? Were you optimistic before you had to deal with cancer?"

Donna replied, "Well, yes, I've always been a person who enjoys life. But I've lived so much better since I had cancer. I don't waste time on things that don't matter. "In fact, I don't go to bed at night until I've had myself a good day!"

The following week, one of the nurses thanked her for her comments during the panel. She added, "I hate to tell

you, Donna, but I stayed up all night trying to make it a
good day!"

"I Am Content . . . "

*Therefore I am content with weaknesses, insults, hard-
ships, persecutions, and calamities for the sake of Christ; for
whenever I am weak, then I am strong.* (2 Cor. 12:10)

YOU care about feeding the hungry.
I need help with my appetite.
Nothing tastes good.
How about doing something for the person
    who is never hungry,
    who can't swallow without gagging?
YOU want people to help the malnourished,
    the undernourished.
How are we to deal with weird diets and fad foods?
I want to take care of my body,
    but it won't respond to my mental commands.
I could lose control, lose all decency.
I want to exercise, but I can't.
I want to develop strength,
    but I may not be able to stand or even sit up.
I long to play golf or tennis, to run or walk.
I need greater therapy than simple exercise.
I need something more than equipment attached,
    something more than devices to lean on or ride.
O GOD, nourish me and build me up—
    spirit, mind, and body.

Mabel's Learnings

Even though Mabel had been through cancer with her mother
and with a college roommate, she knew she needed to
broaden her sensitivity and experience as she began her work
as a psychologist in a cancer center. To help with this prepa-

ration, she invited a dozen cancer survivors, CanCare volunteers, to meet with her and describe "the survivors' world."

She asked them to think of images that picture the initial blow, words and phrases that portray the experience of living with cancer. To prime their imaginations, she led off with "How is living with cancer like taking a ride on a roller coaster?" They immediately identified the emotional ups and downs, the gasps on dangerous curves, the lack of control, the long track, and other features. She gave them a second riddle, alerting them that they were to invent their own riddles next.

"How does the uncertainty and loneliness of cancer resemble being thrown into a strange foreign country?" As they began to answer, their facial expressions told their stories of pain, fear, disorientation, confusion, feeling lost. Quickly they mentioned the difficult language, the mysterious customs and costumes, the need for a guide, not having a passport for security. Soon they were laughing at the idea of being "foreigners."

Then it was the group's turn to formulate riddles. The survivors exploded. Ideas popped like a string of firecrackers. Impromptu questions took shape quickly. "How is living with cancer like— . . . going through a long tunnel and you can't see a light at the end? . . . working on a giant jigsaw puzzle with some of the pieces missing? . . . a ride on a merry-go-round? . . . standing on a trap door? . . . dancing in a minefield? . . . living with a dragon in the closet, and it decides to come out?" "How is finishing a round of chemotherapy like a hiker at the peak of a tall mountain?"

After this session, Mabel made a list of questions she could ask cancer survivors on other occasions: How were you told you had cancer? How do you wish you had been told? Whom did you tell first about your cancer? Why that person? How helpful were that person's reactions? From the doctor's office, through the hospital, to home and your familiar life, who has been helpful in your coping with cancer? What did those persons say or do?

She also made a note: "These survivors can teach all of us about living with uncertainty and confusion and pressure. I'm learning a lot that I didn't get—couldn't get from books or in classrooms."

Dangers and Risks

These fright-filled days, these new developments
    leave us insecure:
What could happen next?
Don't let terror foul us up.
We want to feel stable, content, serene.

YOU provide a strong structure of faith
    for us to lean on and live by.
Thanks!

These beliefs tell us to rely on YOU.
Whether we live or die, we are safe in YOUR love.

Give us courage to face whatever we must,
    the ability to focus on living today well—
    without worrying about what happens next.

While we hate this cancer, we have learned
    to love more
    and
    to draw closer—
to YOU, and
to the people who love us,
to the people we love.
These are treasures!

    Thanks!

Cancer Survivors' Findings

As cancer survivors, we relive the dreadful moments when we found that the monster called cancer had invaded our bodies.

There was no good way for the message to be delivered, no good way for us to respond to the message.

The intensity and variety of reactions stagger us. One person says, "For me it was sheer panic, total alarm!" Another says calmly, "In my case, cancer struck only a glancing blow. It was neither a serious illness nor an emotional trauma."

The earthquake called cancer throws our world into disarray, but the universe doesn't come apart.

We are not alone, though we often feel isolated.

We wonder why, but we go on, even when we can't understand.

We ask about reasons and causes. Even though we don't find satisfying answers, we decide to keep on living.

We find ourselves consumed by fear. At the same time, we are strangely calm and hopeful. We know about mixed emotions.

We affirm that God wants people to be whole, healthy, and happy, but our world is haunted by a terrible killer disease.

We wonder what chances and changes and choices are before us, but we believe that God is in control, that God is suffering with us.

Chapter 2

Making Adjustments

"For me, cancer brought new problems, but it sim-
plified and discarded some old ones that don't bother
me anymore."

"How do I cope? I take my medicine and I pray. I
live one day at a time. Occasionally, I weep and laugh
and pray all at once."

"I'm not the same person I was before cancer. I'm
a better person—tougher and smarter."

Tori's Defiance

Tori and her husband Brent were stunned. Horrible
news piled on top of bad! After surgery to remove a
malignant tumor from her colon, her family doctor sent
her to a large cancer center for additional tests. There
she was to have access to more sophisticated equipment, research, and expertise, which were not available
at local facilities. The couple dropped everything and
went immediately.

After exhaustive tests over several exhausting days,
the experts at the cancer center confirmed her earlier
diagnosis. Her colon cancer, with metastasis to the
liver, was classified as Stage 4. The doctor said bluntly,
"You'll probably live six weeks to six months. Go home
and enjoy. Get back to your family, your teaching, back
to normal living."

They left in a daze. Tori couldn't believe the dismal report. In fact, she declared to Brent, "They can call it denial if they want to, but I refuse to believe it. I feel good, and I have a lot to live for. I have a load of unfulfilled dreams I want to work on, and I want to succeed. Those doctors don't know me or what a fighter I am! I've always thought that we'd have plenty of time to get our girls through school and then take on some of those goals we've talked about." Her husband nodded in agreement, not knowing what options they had but glad to see his wife regaining her optimism.

She named several of her dreams: "We need a preschool at our church, and I'm the one to get it started. It'll take mountains of time and energy, but I want to see that happen. Also, I'll have to rearrange my teaching schedule so I can take that writing course this fall. If I'm ever going to do it, I need to do it now." As she expanded this list of dreams, Brent cheered her on.

While they were driving home, she realized how frightened they both were. At the same time, she felt pressure to squeeze as much out of life as she could. At the top of her expanding list of things to do, she put the name of a friend who had lived five years beyond a similar diagnosis.

Edith responded optimistically to her call. "As your personal, unprofessional adviser, I can assure you that you're right! Those particular doctors, strangers, don't know you or how you'll respond to treatment. Besides, everyone is entitled to additional opinions. Come here and see my oncologist. His positive attitude is contagious, and he uses clinical trials if mainline chemotherapy doesn't work." She reminded Tori, "God gave us life as a gift. God expects us to fight for quality of life. God wants all God's children to be well."

Tori immediately called Edith's oncologist for an appointment. The next day, armed with her records, she and Brent were on a plane, on their way to another consultation. Tori knew that she had found the right physician-partner when he promised her and Brent, "You don't have to fight your battles alone. There's medical help available and I intend to stick with you from now on." The three of them formed an alliance, a partnership for healing. The scheme was for her to have good life as long as possible. He prescribed the chemotherapy, and her cancer journey took a new turn. Tori's spirit soared; she tuned it to the magic of the new oncologist. "I vowed to arrange my life around my treatments and to make my unfulfilled dreams come true—or to die trying!"

Over the next months, she led her church in establishing a weekday preschool. She took a course in creative writing and had an article published in a national magazine. She continued her college teaching and originated a research program for preparing preschool children to learn to read. She supervised student teachers in this project and presented her design to professional groups. She accepted nomination as a candidate for election as an elder in her congregation. She formed a local self-help group for cancer survivors in her hometown. She became a spokesperson for cancer survivors at civic, church, and educational groups.

At their thirtieth wedding anniversary party designed by their children, Brent commented proudly, "Tori, you've managed to make a lot of our dreams come true. And you're feeling great! That's reason to celebrate and thank the Lord."

Six years after the "six weeks to six months" prediction, she reviewed the events of the intervening era. She had surgery six times—colon, liver, twice on her lungs, and twice on her brain. She saw her daughters finish college. She helped plan the older daughter's wedding. She encouraged the younger daughter to go to Africa in the Peace Corps. She helped her son change vocations.

At a luncheon meeting of a civic club in a neighboring town, the program chairman introduced her: "This woman has become a role model for cancer survivors wherever anyone has heard of her. In fact, since her cancer was detected,

she has contributed more to improving the world than most
people do in a lifetime."

More Help, Please

Okay, GOD,
I'm grateful and glad—
    glad that YOU got me through that awful trauma
    at the beginning and brought me this far—
    with a lot of help from
        medicine in all its forms,
        family and friends, strangers too,
        morale builders,
        flowers, notes, cards, gifts, messages,
        wisdom and knowledge from experts,
        prayer, and good sense,
            (so I turned out to be neither foolish nor stupid)
        insurance and money to pay the bills,
        a few people who care and will always be here for me.
YOU know all the other help, all miracles of YOUR grace.
Thanks!

Now YOU and I need to put together and add a fresh set of
help and helpers, some internal and some external:
    a big supply of determination,
    determination for all my helpers too,
    quick relief when I get low,
    drills or exercises that build up body, mind, spirit,
    nerve, so I can be bold and daring,
    sweetness and meanness, to deal with people.
YOU know what I mean.
Feel free to add to my list gifts I don't know to ask for.
Another supply of miracles, I guess.

Let's work together so I can
    put up with unpleasant realities,
    adjust to limits I don't really like,
    rework my dreams and expectations,

adopt immediate and long-range goals,
enjoy each day, maybe even its rough spots,
live well despite my frustrations and burdens,
encourage someone else, even when I'm discouraged,
thrive on my alone time, with YOU.

Let me know what else we need to work on together. Okay?

These are moves YOU and I need to make,
toward what they call "Adjusting."
Let's keep at it, please. Amen.

The Trio's Harmony

Ms. Lamb explained to new arrivals in the waiting room at the radiation clinic, "In this corner of the waiting room, you are welcome. We call ourselves 'The Trio,' because usually you can expect three of the gang to be here. You see, we have our own way of counting. Some patients are here daily, others once or twice a week, so this corner may seat five or six people, but we're still 'The Trio'. Please join us."

On one occasion, Ms. Lamb led the conversation into a serious zone by asking, "How would you answer the question, 'How do you keep going when you're dealing with a deadly disease?'"

"Well," Ms. James started cautiously, "my sister and my husband were my strong right arm—and both legs, when I couldn't stand on my own. Neighbors and friends were not as panicky as I expected them to be; in fact, they were clever and helpful. They treated me like a real person with a big problem, not like a freak wearing the cancer label."

The newcomer spoke up: "My main problem is all the changes I've had to adjust to—loss of hair, physical therapy that strains me, adjusting my work schedule so I can keep my treatments on track and on time, and explaining to my kids why I can't do all the things they expect. My most important help came from a counselor. She helped me see that I was adjusting to a new self-image."

Mickey blurted out, "Well, I couldn't have made it without my little pooch Pheobe. She kept me going all through this mess. I also got help from other cancer survivors who let me chatter and weep or moan or giggle about my feelings and about all the strange things on my mind. I hope I can help other people that way someday."

After an awkward silence, Lucille spoke. "In The Trio we haven't talked a lot about religion or faith, but I don't see how anyone with cancer can live or die without some kind of spiritual foundation. I'm talking about sensing God's presence in the hospital or when I'm alone or with people who care. The folks in my church have held me up by praying and by the kindness you were talking about. I find that prayer and worship are as important to me as food and medicine—all gifts from the Great Healer!

"But the new thing I've found is that my search for meaning is a sacred enterprise. I don't believe that God sent cancer into our lives, but I'm sure God has used this occasion to help me grow into a stronger, more useful person."

The five people soon disbanded for the day. They never admitted that they held meetings or made group decisions of any kind. But they were members of a body, players in The Trio.

Secrets

All-knowing GOD,
Secrets are a problem now.
There are things—
    facts, ideas,
    dreams, feelings, a few memories—
    that I need to keep to myself,
        as I guard my privacy.

Everyone doesn't need to know everything.
　　Data can be dangerous.
　　Ideas can do harm.
　　Dreams can mislead.
　　Feelings can do damage.
　　Memories can be mistaken.

But,
I don't want them keeping secrets from me,
　　to overprotect me.

If they keep me from knowing,
they don't let me
　　decide what to do,
　　fight as I need to,
　　enjoy what I can,
　　love, in time that is precious.

So, please help us be honest and help us be kind.
I want to know what I need to know,
I need to tell them what they need to know.

All this makes love difficult now.

Show us how to handle secrets, please.

Planning

GOD of the future, as well as the past and the present:

As I'm looking ahead at the rest of my life,
I hope the months or years will not be all *rest*.

I hope to do some things that are worthwhile,
　　to build on what's happened before,
　　to fill time with work and play.
　　to make some dreams come true,
　　to heal leftover wounds,
　　to follow good urges,
　　to pick up what I've put off,
　　to love and be loved.

It's hard to make plans
when necessary components are missing now.
   I wonder if old motivations can still shove me along.
   I hope I can count on some time,
      for me to heal and to help someone else.
   I long to use the knowledge, interests, and skills
      that might have been taken away.
   I want to make a difference in this tired old world.

But I need to look ahead,
   to set some immediate and long-term goals,
      and to accomplish a good load of them,
   to treasure the days and years as they unfold,
      while I find nourishment in good memories,
   to relish time with people I love,
   to enjoy reunions,
   to find ways of being useful,
   to grow and think a lot and to travel some,
   to repair damaged relationships,
   to find satisfaction in things I can do,
   to leave the ultimate future
      in YOUR powerful love.

Neil's Ties! Carla's Therapy!

After a slow recovery from surgery, Carla was left with a weight of uncertainty that she couldn't lift or carry with dignity. Her restraints collapsed under the weight, so she treated herself to periods of private rage. She timed them when no one else was in the house. She chose the bedroom as the proper place.

As her instruments, Carla selected a mound of small, soft decorative pillows along with the wall full of ties in her husband Neil's closet. She vented her pent-up frustrations in an hour of shouting and wailing. She slung the bands of color around, like a frenzied cheerleader waving pompoms. She tossed pillows at the windows, flinging them across the room, dashing from corner to corner, racing to stir up any clutter that seemed to settle down or to escape her grasp. She allowed nothing to rest in peace. A whirling dervish, she filled the room with sound and fury. The messier the scene, the bolder she became, until she was exhausted, overstuffed on her feast of frenzy. With her tornado of spinning ties and her explosion of flying pillows, she trashed the bedroom. However, she did no real harm; she caused only temporary damage, easy to repair.

After a sigh of relief and a quiet cup of coffee, she realized that her psyche had flushed out its rage. Her energy was used up, and she felt clean inside.

The therapy was valuable, she reflected, and it had been cost-free. More important, her psyche came out more tidy than the room she used and abused. Before her next conference with her therapist, she could decide how to report this incident to the counselor or to her husband. She thought, "Both of them may be proud that I've invented a cheap form of therapy, an original method of self-treatment. I'll make a note to remind myself that the spontaneous technique worked and that the scene and materials are available if and when I need them again."

Roy Magee's Claim

Roy went through a lot before he found the right words to describe his battle with cancer. Great chunks of his life had been fights—fighting his way out of the black ghetto, struggling through college and law school with minimal support from his family. "They couldn't help anyway," he said. "Then I invaded this city already full of successful white lawyers."

On the other hand, Roy described other aspects of his life as "unbelievable gifts—my intelligent, successful, glamorous professor wife, our teenage daughter whom I adore, my thriving law practice, and our comfortable home in a prestigious neighborhood, the farthest away from ghetto life."

The diagnosis of colon cancer knocked him down temporarily. But he regained his footing after surgery and bounced back for more fight. Months later, the discovery of metastatic disease in other parts of his body again laid him low emotionally. "This time," he said, "the antihuman tests, the constant treatments, and the miserable side effects dragged me down and stomped on me." The physical ailments, the endless waiting for another round, the depressing prospects—all these blows put him down for a long count.

As the disease seemed to be winning, a friend asked how he would describe his whole situation. Roy answered as though he had rehearsed for this conversation: "I've done a lot of thinking about what's happening to me, and what I have to say is this. Man, I'm too young, too smart, and too good-looking to have to put up with this mess!"

A Question, about Courage

Cancer cripples!
Cancer causes collapse!
Cancer creates consternation!
How
can I be brave
or
even content?
The treatments
leave me disoriented.
I see myself
battered and bloody,
crippled and worried,
frenzied and fearful.
People I love are

being damaged.
Others leave me alone.
People I don't know
throw pity at me.
How can I be brave?
Content?
Grace!?
Yes? Yes! Okay!

Kendall's Candy

Kendall enjoyed his reputation as a successful businessman. Around the medical center they called him "the Candy Man." He carried candy in the pockets of his sports jacket or his bathrobe, and he gave it away generously. He made purchases by the case from a firm that supplied classy restaurants. He reported, "This is my contribution to morale in the whole hospital. Doctors and nurses need as big a boost as patients and visitors."

He found that he had become famous for his ways of dealing with colon cancer and for his recovery after each operation. "I don't wait for the therapists to tell me to get up and walk. I get on my feet ahead of schedule, before I feel like it, with or without assistance."

Kendall didn't really like the idea of visiting other people who were having a hard time with cancer. "But I realize that I've been helped in good ways, so I couldn't say no to the CanCare volunteer who asked me to talk with Bob. She explained that Bob was a professor, that he was lonely, away from home, and that he had bad news about his illness. I didn't want to do the official 'visit' pattern. I've seen too many visitors bothering patients by hanging around, getting in the way. I didn't want to do that sort of thing, so I called Bob and asked him to go for a drive."

The two men talked for an hour as Kendall showed Bob points of interest around town. Both enjoyed the outing.

The counselor commended Kendall: "You really helped Bob."

"Well," said Kendall, "I don't understand how that works. Maybe I'll give it another try, if you need me sometime. But you know, I'm a lot more comfortable giving away candy."

Friends

GOD,
YOU know what it's like to be alone,
    to lose the people YOU care about.
Help me take initiatives with my friends.
    I want to help them reach into and through
    the confusion, so we can communicate again.

The cancer hides me, but it hasn't blotted me out.
    I want them to touch me without cringing.
    I want them to look at me without showing pity for me.
    I want them to hear me without listening for death rattles.

I want to help them to understand my condition
    and to make contact,
    so we can continue to be in touch.
I want to help them know that the disease is not contagious.
I want them to avoid cancer-causing risks.
I want to help them find meanings for life,
    before their lives are threatened.
I want to help my friends and
I want them to help me.

A Non-Patient's Prayer

GOD,
YOU know how it is to hurt for and with someone YOU love.
That's where I am now.

I want to take away the pain, the discomfort,
    the inconvenience, the misery,

but all I can do is stand here or pace the floor,
   and wring my hands
      and pray.

Help me hold up.
I want my being here to be a help, not a burden.
Work through me so this precious person
   won't have to work so hard.

YOU built us so we can bear one another's burdens.
Now, build me up so I'll have the strength to be helpful,
   so I'll say and do something worthwhile,
      even though I can't figure out
      what to say or do.

YOU know too
   that I want this disease conquered and removed
   from people I love.
I want it conquered and banished
   from the world YOU love.
Let me have a hand in destroying this destroyer. Please.

These Men's Prostates

Casey's sister called to ask about Casey's physician husband, Harris, and his recovery from prostate surgery. "What about the surgery and how is his recovery going?"

Casey answered, "Oh, the surgery was highly successful. But let me tell you what happened last night. If I remember correctly, he called it 'a meeting of the Not-so-Secret or Mysterious Fraternity of the Malfunctioning Prostate.' The gathering last night was really a patient education session led by his surgeon friend and the urologist he likes. He said they didn't have a secret initiation ceremony, just a pair of informative lectures and a few questions. He said they covered the latest developments in treatment without promising too much and without discouraging the patients. They explained that nearly all men in their later years have enlarged prostate glands.

"What he talked about most was the group he sat with. One had his prostate removed and had fought depression over his impotence. A younger man talked about 'the roto-rooter job' he had, but he didn't have cancer. Oh, they call it TURP—TransUrethral Resection of the Prostate. Another has a high PSA count, and he's had biopsies but no reports of malignancy. Harris said they talked openly about everything, about impotence, incontinence, and how many diapers each uses a day. Can you believe Harris could be serious throughout the whole evening? But it's clear that he's joined the fraternity he had ridiculed."

She paused for a question from her sister, then answered, "Yes, there were wives present, but not in his group. And no, I don't plan to attend with him, and I don't expect him to invite me.

"I've been thinking about his clowning around. Sometimes the foolishness scares people. They may think he can't be serious or caring, but his humor covers his embarrassment or his discomfort about people who are not well. So maybe he holds back and uses that humor as healthy treatment, not an unhealthy diversion or denial or escape mechanism."

Worry Shatters Joy

Generous and patient GOD:

Good news today, and I thank YOU,
    but I've let worry rob me of gladness at this moment.
Worry can cause me to borrow trouble I may never meet.
Now, I'm reflecting on the mix of emotions I carry:
I need to feel as secure as the tests tell me I am.
I want to be in a mood of celebration,
    but I'm afraid to tempt fate.
I don't really believe that some eternal system of justice will
    resent my joy and retaliate by zapping me with more pain,
    to balance an obsolete set of scales.

So, why am I so uncertain,
    so insecure,
    so cautious,
    so danger-shy,
    so fear-driven?
My pattern of recovery has been encouraging,
    my tests reveal progress in my health,
    my family and friends
        could not be more concerned
            or more helpful in my crisis.

YOU have made me aware of YOUR presence
    all through the ordeal of cancer.
I also need YOU to protect me from dumb superstitions,
    from panic at minor setbacks, and
    from being haunted by bad events that are over and gone.

I want a carefree spirit so I can enjoy this new life YOU
    are opening up for us now.
Help me be joyful in my gratitude so I can
    celebrate each day as a new creation,
    find or invent rituals that express thanks for YOUR
    gift of life.

I want to be sensible. I want to be bold. I want to be daring.
Help me do and think and feel and believe everything
    I need to do and think and feel and believe.
And I want to enjoy all the good gifts YOU give.
Please empower gratitude to override my worries.

Dixon's Fury

Dixon told his CanCare training class exactly how he got through his initial cancer experience—lymphoma of the brain. He said, "I was so angry at the disease, the treatments, the doctors, the clumsy tests, my whole situation. I was mad at everyone and everything." He explained further that he was in a group of fifteen patients with the same disease, the same experimental protocol for treatment, and he was the only one who survived. He recalled that he was just too furious to let cancer get to him. Of course, he went on to tell that it cost him his job, his marriage, and valuable time with his small children. In fact, all his dreams were either drastically changed or put on hold.

Dixon took a weekend of CanCare intensive training. With this group of volunteers, Dixon learned to offer friendship, and to help other persons dealing with brain cancer. In the training class, he was taught not to expect others to cope with the disease the way he had. "Now, I see that there's no one right or wrong way to deal with cancer. Each of us finds his own way. I can still help people by being there and listening to their stories. This helps them focus on getting through the bad times and celebrating the good times. I do know how to do that part."

Ten years into his new life after the cancer diagnosis, he was taking care of assigned survivors while also taking care of his business from his home, seeing his children twice a week, and playing tennis often. "I met and married a fabulous optimistic woman who was not afraid of my cancer history." Life had taken a good turn. Dixon felt that he was "home free." Then the lymphoma attacked again. This time, the disease was in his eye. It was a devastating blow.

However, he had spent ten years helping other survivors deal with brain cancer. He had a lovely supportive wife who would never back away. He also had a group of men friends at his church who set up a schedule and took turns driving him across town for daily treatment so his wife would not need to leave her job.

He had eye surgery, a lens implant, surgery to remove fluid, three rounds of chemotherapy, and radiation. Three years later, thirteen years after his original diagnosis, he was still on Interferon and getting shaky reports. In fact, all his doctors at the cancer center were amazed that he was doing so well. They couldn't understand how he was still functioning at such a high level. He was wishing for greater encouragement from them.

Dixon admitted that his quality of life was not as strong as it had been three years earlier. However, he was driving, operating his office from home, and playing tennis or golf a couple of times a week.

He said, "Now my wife regularly beats me at tennis. When I'm tired, I notice my speech is fuzzy. But I don't feel bad, and life is good!" Dixon was certain this time that the prayers of many people and his peaceful, happy life had brought him to this new level.

He commented, "I've got my priorities in order. I love my wife and children, and I want all the quality time I can get with them. I don't want to spend time on things that don't matter or that cause stress. I know I get energy from reaching out to others, so I will always want to be involved with other cancer survivors."

Dixon and his wife continued to put emphasis on living well. Even while he was in treatment, they invited twenty people to a party at his home to honor a hospital chaplain and his bride. The chaplain had been a close friend through three difficult years and helped Dixon again put cancer in its place.

Survival

GOD,
YOU and I may be the only ones who regard this as a prayer, but here goes.

I'm wondering if survival is a worthy purpose for living.
It doesn't claim any benefit except for the person surviving.
Don't get me wrong, I want to keep on living,
But good living, decent living, includes unselfish elements, right?

I want to survive so I can take care of my family, my work, to "live up" the years I'm given and

to make a difference in the world,
    to contribute.

Yes, I may be influencing people
    without being aware of my impact.
YOU've taught me that I'm not responsible for results,
    only for love and faithfulness,
        with good intentions and holy thoughts along the way.
Sure, I want to accomplish,
    to be respected and to be respectable.

And, one way and another,
YOU have been showing me that
    I can do most of these whether I'm sick or well.

But I would like to have a chance
    to do these important things
        when I'm feeling better than I do now.

I know YOU are not keen about making deals.
YOU and I know how I feel about all of this.

The best I can offer is my desire
    to live and to do something more than survive—
    for YOU, for myself,
        for the people we love, for the whole world.

I think I'm ready to get going.
Coping with the disease is not enough to satisfy YOU or me.
I don't have to figure out
    whether this qualifies as a prayer or not.

YOU decide.
Amen!

Mabel's Hearing

After several lunchtime conversations with her gathered group of survivors, Mabel was feeling better prepared to work as a psychologist in the cancer center.

In one session, she asked the members of the group to tell her how they see themselves, not how the world views them but how they might describe themselves to a soul mate. She noted their comments:

"I need to be seen as a *person* first—then as a cancer patient."

"I feel different—different from everyone else and different from what I was last week."

"I'm suffering loss, and I'm often lonely."

"I feel like a cog in the giant medical machine. I've lost most of my dignity."

"I'm confronting my mortality, wrestling with ultimate meanings."

"I hate this disease and what it has done to turn my world upside down. I hate what it does to people I love."

"Like everyone else, I have a long 'want list'—hope and optimism, joy and humor, dreams and visions."

"I need to focus attention on living rather than dying, on giving rather than getting."

"I still have interests in the larger world, but I feel separated from it."

"I care about the people around me."

"I'm afraid, frustrated, worried. My resources for coping are limited and they're almost used up."

"I can't stop asking 'Why?' But I don't like any of the answers I get."

"I want to believe that God is in control, but I don't understand why life is such a mess; and I don't like the way things are going."

"I want and need to pray, but it's hard to do."

Mabel realized that they were articulating messages they would have liked to scream at the world.

Cancer Survivors' Findings

We're like performers in a circus. We cancer survivors do daring things, take risks, learn by discipline and practice, and we're constantly watched. We don't put our heads into the mouths of vicious animals or perform over a safety net, but we do walk on tightropes and depend on support teams. We could keep going with these analogies—we fly through the air like trapeze artists, we wear strange garb, we march in colorful parades.

Normally, we cancer survivors don't get public acclaim. We can't practice for our most dramatic moments. Impromptu or with minimum warnings or preparation, we show up for exhausting, life-threatening procedures. Although the cancer world restricts and confuses us, we have varied reactions and adjustments, unique personal styles, and complicated networks of concern.

We live under pressure. Both circus performers and cancer survivors occupy worlds that tend to isolate them. But lively spirits manage to stay connected with the larger world.

Cancer survivors perform in three rings at the same time—the physical, the emotional or mental, and the spiritual.

Everybody in this parade is hoping to live as long as possible and as fully as possible.

Chapter 3

Confronting Other Forces

*"When you have cancer, you have to deal with prob-
lems and temptations and frustrations. In fact, all of
them get more aggravating when you have cancer."*

*"Why do I, the sick person dealing with cancer,
have to comfort my friends who are upset by my cancer? Why do we have to be the ones who work for re-
forms for the benefit of people with cancer? Can anyone else speak out for us? Who are our advocates?"*

Transplanting

Generous GOD:
YOU have seen to it
    that we develop wisdom and skills
        through various disciplines and
        through tough experiences,
        in crisis times.

While we carry this cancer cargo,
    we need to activate our accumulated tools.

I need to remember
    that YOU and I together
    have dealt with tough stuff before.

Give me good sense now
    to take inventory and
    to use wisdom from the past,

lessons learned along the way,
skills sharpened in brighter times,
ability to adjust,
creativity for challenging situations.

An organ transplant is not what I need.
Thank YOU very much for that.
I do need to reclaim, recycle, redevelop,
   transplant and use
     all these resources
   so YOU and I can outlive the dangers and
     conquer this demon called "cancer"
     for others and for myself.

Cancer, Family, and the Outside World

Look, GOD, YOU and I want me to get well.
Whether I'm well or not,
I have things that matter to me,
   and I want to give them attention.
My family needs me.
Each child deserves my time and consideration.
My spouse wants and should get
   partnership with me.
Other family members also suffer from neglect.
These ties and my friends require concentration.
   I don't want to fail any of them.
   I want to focus on these dear people.
Let's not let cancer dominate my mind and heart.

The world is moving ahead whether I'm sick or well.
   News reports can be discouraging, alarming,
   but I have to stay in touch.
Other people can carry my usual workload,
   while I appear to be loafing, or feel that I'm loafing.
Civic life, citizenship call me to service,
   but I'm no help to anyone or any cause now.
Let's not let cancer kill my concerns, shrink my world.

My spirit is ailing, my mental and spiritual stamina has
   slumped.
Praying helps, but I'm not very good at it.
YOUR presence makes me strong,
   even when my prayers stumble.
Maybe I expect magic to work when I do holy things.
Help me see that waiting in quietness
   and confidence
   is also good medicine for my soul.

I really want to carry on my responsibilities.
At the same time, I don't want to focus on my needs
   more than I focus on
      YOU and YOUR greatness,
      on YOUR grace available in all these concerns.

YOU and I need to straighten me out. Help me cooperate.
Please, and thank YOU.

Mary Carol's Colostomy

At the twentieth anniversary reunion of her nursing school
class, Carol talked freely with her classmates.

"You girls know about my husband, Corey, and my children, Hank and Emily. Now I'm going to tell you about the
newest member of the family—my colostomy. We named
him Willie. He became a member of the family two years ago
when I had surgery for colorectal cancer. I don't have to use
an external bag, but I do have to spend forty-five minutes
every morning having intimate relations with Willie. The
workouts with Willie take place immediately after morning
prayers.

"Six months after my operation, when Corey and I took a
cruise, I was bold enough to wear my two-piece swimsuit on
the beach. There were no disasters. No whistles or requests
for autographs!

"You're probably curious—most people seem to be—
about sex for Corey and me, with Willie in the picture. That

was a difficult but fairly brief adjustment. It wasn't like 'Don't come near me,' or 'I don't want you to see it.' Nothing that deadly or serious, but there was this thing on my side. I have few inhibitions, but it still bothered me. Now Corey knew all about it and we were very open, but I was uncomfortable mentally the first few times we made love. Corey said it didn't bother him at all. And even though he said that, I think he was afraid of hurting me. Now when we're alone together, Willie doesn't bother us at all. It's like Willie isn't even there.

"If they'd tried to teach us about these things in nursing school, would we have believed them? I don't think so. I'm not sure I believe them now, and they've happened to me!"

Laurel's Anger

Dr. Webster chuckled as he walked out of the examining room, leaving his new patient Laurel. "If she's got that much fire left in her, she can use some of it to fight cancer!"

At the beginning of the interview, Laurel complained that the medicine made her nauseated. He sensed that her upset had a broader, deeper basis. He asked what was causing her distress, besides the medicine. She gave him a complicated account of what the insurance companies and the bookkeepers in the doctors' offices back home had done to her. "They seem to pick on us poor widow women," she complained. The doctor listened closely, encouraging her anger to come out as she told the story. The more she talked, the more fire she showed. She was refusing to pay bills, the ones she knew were unfair.

Dr. Webster continued the examination. At the same time, she continued to talk. He gave her plenty of time to vent her feelings. He explained the change he was making in her prescriptions, shifting away from the drugs that caused her nausea. With the comment, "Vomiting is a hellish way to live," he promised that the new medicine wouldn't make her sick. If it did, he would find another.

He was pleased with himself but more pleased with her. He liked her fury. He thought, "She's been hiding it—from herself and from her family. I want her to use it along with the chemotherapy. She'll figure out how, and we can give her some coaching."

Elmer's Medical Bills

Elmer had to give up his job as houseparent for delinquent boys when his cancer was diagnosed. He had been out of college for only a few months. As a new staff member in a non-profit service, he had no insurance to cover the costs of treatment. His health problems became quite complicated. His treatments were prolonged, expensive, and extensive. He was hospitalized for weeks. "My bills were enormous—thousands and thousands of dollars!" he exclaimed.

Several months after Elmer's release from the cancer center, the hospital enclosed a curt note with his bill, insisting that he pay the staggering amount he owed. At the time, he was living with his parents. He was unable to work.

Elmer wrote across the bottom of the hospital's letter, "I have no income, and I owe a lot for college debts. My only possessions are a dog and an old pickup. Come get them."

Ethical Issues

Look here, GOD:

While this cancer is gnawing at me,
I also have a load of issues to deal with:

I have to be considerate of the feelings of others.

Being good and being a patient don't fit together;

I'm long on self-pity, short on patience.

It's hard to solve problems
    when there seem to be no answers that are
    fully right or clearly wrong,
    purely good or completely bad.

Someone else, or some giant system
    has already decided or will decide
        whether drugs will be available,
        who can get or afford treatments,
        who takes care and who gives care and
        who gives a damn.

And, on a more personal level,
    who decides what happens to me,
    who takes care of me,
    when I'm not able to make decisions?

Now that I'm becoming alert to all these issues,
    I need YOU and
    I need one or more human beings
        to help me think all this through
        and to help carry through.

Please watch me while I'm dealing with
    matters that are too much for me.
Watch with me so I make good decisions,
    even though I make mistakes and
    even when I am mistreated by mistakes.

Maude's Dilemma

"I've dated Carl for several weeks," Maude told her friend Rachel as she began a one-sided conversation. "I'm having to wrestle with my principles while I decide how I feel about him. At this point, neither of us has said that we are in love or that we want our ties to become serious or permanent. But he wants me to go to bed with him. Thanks for not showing shock—or disgust!"

Both women took a deep breath, then Maude continued. "He tells me that he has cancer and that he needs me. His parents are both dead. He's in his early thirties. He has never married, and he's not close to his brother. He doesn't want anyone at his office to know that he has cancer. He's says that I'm the only one who knows or cares.

"He's been generous. When my car broke down, he bought a second car and told me I could use it indefinitely. I don't want to pity him. Neither do I want him to try to take advantage of my goodwill. But he won't even tell me who his local doctor is. He won't talk about his feelings or give any details about his cancer or the treatments.

"We do have a lot in common. We like the outdoors. We both read a lot; we don't watch television. He hasn't met any of my friends, and I don't know whether he has any.

"If I'm the only person he talks with, how can I leave him stranded with this terrible disease? That's my quandary, my worry."

Rachel thought to herself, "Maude hasn't asked what I think, but I'm afraid she's in danger. I'm afraid she's taking on too much when this guy's not sharing much with her—except that car."

Maude interrupted Rachel's train of thought, "Can this ever be a healthy romance with an unhealthy man? Can I be sure that he has cancer? And if he does, how long can he live? Am I avoiding something great, or am I fascinated with something disastrous? I'm on treacherous footing, and I don't know which way to turn."

Jo's Workplace

Fresh out of college, Jo was the newest employee in the firm. After less than a year, she discovered a lump in her breast that turned out to be malignant. She was expected to live only a few months.

She wasn't able to have surgery, but she was to spend two hours daily at the clinic. She was to undergo chemotherapy each afternoon, along with radiation each morning. The procedures were to continue for weeks, even months, possibly a year.

She told her employer that she was ready to work doubly hard through long hours to meet her quotas, to keep her sales up. She found that he expected her to give up her position. He told Jo that he was sorry to lose her from the sales force.

Jo fired back at him, "Just a minute now! I'm not resigning. I want to keep working. I have no insurance and I don't want to be dependent on my folks again. Yes, I'll have to be away from work several hours every day. I won't be feeling good. I may not look good either. But I intend to keep up my quotas, to do a good job. If I don't keep up, you'll be justified in firing me. But if you fire me without giving me a chance, I'll take you to court. And I think I'll win."

Jo was able to tolerate the treatments. She held up under the pressures of a contorted work schedule. Her sales record surpassed her expectations. In fact, during her six months of treatment, her totals were better than in the previous six months. Two years later, her boss boasted, "Jo's our star performer. And she kept going even when she was having cancer treatments!"

Five years later, Jo stated, "The treatments were effective! I got through them without losing my job. I developed a lot of self-confidence, so I'm proud to call myself a survivor—a healthy cancer survivor!"

Moving Ahead

GOD of all healing and health:

Now that I'm able to move back into normal patterns of living, it's good not to have
 all that attention centered on me and my disease.

It's great to be back in the land of the living!
Hallelujah!

But I wonder if I'll have to tell people,
even if they don't ask about it,
    that I'm afflicted,
    that I too am in that awful category—
        handicapped, incapacitated, unhealthy.

Maybe, if I can talk about it openly
and can practice what I need to say and
how to say it,
    then the people I talk with will be more kind
    to the voiceless cancer patients,
    who can't or don't speak up for themselves.
Help me to be an advocate for my brothers and sisters.
Please.

Rob's New Mission

At first, after a biopsy of his lung, Rob was told that he had to have surgery to remove a portion of one lung. "That didn't sound good, but it didn't sound too bad. I was in good health. I could handle it."

The day before the operation, he and his wife Jennifer had a bigger jolt. Lab reports showed that the malignancy had reached beyond the lung and had affected the lymph system. Surgery could not solve the whole problem. New plans called for him to go through radiation after surgery. The treatments worked!

He looked back later, amused that he had been so bothered about the loss of his hair. "Maybe that worry over a trivial thing protected my mind from thinking about worse things. Jennifer convinced me that she didn't care whether I had hair or not. She was a great strong support through the whole process. She focused all her energy and attention on me and my recovery. Together we made it!"

Four years later, the main feelings he remembered were loneliness and weakness—physical, emotional, spiritual, social. "I hope no one else ever has to go through that kind of experience again.

"That's why both of us get such a kick out of talking with other cancer people—husbands and wives going through the maze and needing a friendly touch for encouragement."

Confrontation

GOD of all people:
Now that I'm one of the survivors,
I want to help others who have cancer.

Parts of the task can be done by
    gentle good deeds among ourselves.
We can also help the public
    allow us cancer people to live normal lives
        in the so-called normal world,
    treat us like normal people with a dreadful disease.

These ideas make me realize that I may have to work at it.
We may have to become a pressure group,
    to become politically active,
    to engage in lobbying.
I'm not comfortable with confrontation, but I know that
    if we cancer people stick together
    we can change this world.

We have to agitate
    to correct wrongful situations, rules, regulations
    that hamper research, recovery, rehabilitation.

We are a big crowd, but all of us don't pull together.
Even a small number of us, carefully focused,
    could make a big difference,
    make a big splash.

We can also wield influence
    by conversation and interpretation and instruction.

Lawrence's Isolation

Lawrence, a middle management executive in his bank, was reviewing six months' experience with cancer. He and his wife, Cheryl, were making the most of a rare weekend away from routine.

"These six months haven't been nearly as bad as I was expecting them to be. First, all of us in the office laughed about the bank sponsoring a screening for colon cancer. Several joked that the top executives had already passed the test; now they were checking to see who might have problems taking on more responsibility and living with more stress. They teased that this test was really to see who could move on up the corporate ladder. It was a joke then. It ceased to be funny when several of us were advised to see our doctors for more thorough testing. I was never aware of any bleeding, but that miserable little hemocult test announced it loud and clear."

"I'm glad they pushed that testing," said Cheryl.

"Sure! I am too," affirmed Lawrence. "You and I managed not to go into alarm or to cause the children to be alarmed when it was confirmed that the tumor in my colon was malignant. We stayed pretty calm, I thought, especially when we told our families what was going on. Maybe we made a mistake by letting everyone know, by coming out of the closet about the Big C. Right away it became public information, that I had cancer and that I was taking chemotherapy to get ready for the operation. That's when I noticed that people at work were beginning to treat me differently. They acted like I had gone away, like I wasn't there any more. In fact, I didn't have anyone to talk with—about sports or anything, certainly not my health. They acted as though I was someone they didn't know.

"At the same time, the official reactions were as helpful as they could be. I was assured that all of us would be taken care of, that I should take off from work whenever I needed to have treatment, and that I should not feel bad about taking time off when I was just feeling crummy. The personnel people explained all about the insurance and the policies on taking care of employees and their families when there is a health crisis. The organization and my supervisors were quite helpful and concerned.

"The problem all along has been with my colleagues—buddies I had always had lunch with, the ones who used to stop and chat as they moved around our section of the building. Now I feel that all the old gang have turned their backs on me. Some of the higher-ups avoid me too. One guy actually looks at the floor when we are on the elevator together. He stutters if I try to start a conversation with him. So I quit trying.

"You know how we all keep our doors open into the outer area unless we really need privacy? I liked the professional but chummy atmosphere. No longer! No one stops casually while moving around the area. We used to take coffee breaks together."

Cheryl invited him to talk more about his feelings, "You miss that, don't you?"

"Maybe I'm paranoid now, but I see some of these people taking the long way around through the area to avoid coming close to my door. As far as I can tell, no one goes to lunch with anyone else in the office any longer. Or, if we eat at our desks, no two people get together. At least, if anyone feels close to anyone else in our outfit, I don't know about it. I'm not included."

Cheryl hadn't felt shut out, so she reminded him, "The wives have been gracious when I've had contact with them."

"Yes," Lawrence admitted, "we did get cards and notes from some of the folks—mostly to you from other wives. And we had more attention in the immediate crisis. But that was months ago. When and how can we convince all these people that I'm healthy, that I'm the same guy I always was?

I've made it a point to tell a lot of them that I had that series of chemotherapy treatments to shrink the tumor before surgery. The explanation went out in memos announcing what the surgeon found. The tumor was minute because the chemo was effective. That's why the surgery was so simple. My recovery went well, and I was back at work promptly, part-time at first and then full-time within a month. But the aftereffects on our social life and on my personal relations at work are shot. My self-esteem is down. All this psychological isolation is painful. Those damages may be permanent."

"I hope they're not permanent," said Cheryl. She saw that they needed a plan. "What can we do about all this now? Got any ideas?"

Lawrence couldn't think of anything constructive. After another pause, he went on. "I don't want to put a notice in the employees' newsletter announcing that I'm now a healthy, happy, wholesome person. I don't want to make an official request that people be nice to me. I only want a normal chance to live a normal life and to have normal friends who treat me like a normal human being. Am I wanting and expecting too much? What can I do, what can we do, to change all this?"

"Would this be the time for you to talk to the human services people?" Cheryl interrupted. "Maybe someone there could make a suggestion or be an advocate for you if they knew about the problems you're having. How about that new guy who is your immediate supervisor? You said that the administration has been attentive and kind all the way through. How about letting someone at that level know all this?"

Lawrence was glad to talk openly with Cheryl, but he was still deeply discouraged. "Maybe I ought to ask for a transfer and bury this as part of our past. But I really don't want to uproot the kids or go through that drastic change. A move

shouldn't be necessary. What else can we do? What can anyone do?"

Malpractice? Maybe

GOD of justice and rightness:

After this latest incident,
I was advised that
I could sue someone for malpractice
    and get a generous settlement.

How do I know whether it is malpractice—
    or an honest but harmful mistake,
    or serious incompetence,
    or an unavoidable incident which is no one's fault,
    or something else I haven't thought about?

What good would it do to go to court
    while I'm completely occupied with recovering?

They tell me that attorneys and insurance people
    have made malpractice into a profitable industry.
Who profits?
Do I benefit really? Who does—other patients, later?
Who pays—what persons and what institutions?
Who can be damaged further
    if I do or if I don't take it to court?

What good will it do me, or anyone else
    if I should lose?—or if I should win?

How much stamina, already in limited supply,
    can I afford to invest?

I don't like the idea,
    unless something worse happens,
    unless I can be more certain about answering these
        questions, solving these riddles,
    unless I can feel some peace about these issues.

Tired of questions? So am I. What's next?

What's fair? What's just? For them and for me?

YOU are working through all this with me, aren't YOU?

Cancer Survivors' Findings

We who live in the cancer world also occupy other overlapping, sometimes competing worlds. If the cancer survivors portrayed in this section were newsmakers, headlines might read as follows: "Cancer Survivor Accuses Employer of Job Discrimination," "Survivor Is Victim of Social Ostracism in Workplace," "Experienced Nurse Reveals Life with Ostomy," "Youthful Cancer Survivor Offers Dog and Truck to Pay Medical Bills," "Cancer Survivors Meet Ethical Issues, Personal, and Political."

In addition to our traumatic experience, we cancer survivors deal with everyday realities—politics, finances, family, work, play, religion, business, and education.

We cancer survivors can panic when we meet ordinary difficulties. A headache becomes a catastrophic threat—signaling a spread to the brain from another part of the body or an attack by a new tumor. Because cancer intensifies many aspects of life, a burp or a cough can cause alarm. The initial trauma leaves wounds and aftereffects.

On the other hand, the cancer experience intensifies and amplifies familiar or new values. Because of cancer, we survivors make fresh commitments and repair damaged relations. Or we decide to treasure, modify, strengthen the connections that enrich us and the people around us. We are grateful for new life and its delights; we address our gratitude to God and to people close by.

Chapter 4

Managing the Healing Team

"Some people volunteered to be on my healing team. I hired others. Sometimes I'm the captain or coach. At other times I'm only a member of the team."

"My doctor's office has a cool sampler on the wall. It says, 'God does the healing. The doctor collects the fees.'"

"I discovered that I have to trust my doctor. It helps that we like each other."

Delaney's Wedding Flowers

Delaney and Paul's friendship grew into a college romance and blossomed as a marriage. They spent a summer studying at Oxford in England. By graduation, they were planning their marriage.

Delaney and Paul talked at length about their childhood and growing-up years. He was curious and encouraging when she told him about her Hodgkin's disease, diagnosed three years before they met. She was relieved that the story didn't scare him away.

Their wedding day approached. She had passed the milestone, her five years after diagnosis. She remembered those heavy times along the way. She and Paul had heart-to-heart talks about the permanent "question mark" hanging over her health. Paul was calm about the cancer shadow that would follow them into their future together.

They invited friends and relatives to be members of the wedding party. Each chose attendants who had been friends in high school or college. They selected as readings two pieces of poetry from their literature course in England.

Delaney was trying to think of a suitable way to include the cancer experience in the ceremony when she remembered that her favorite doctor grew orchids as a hobby. She made an appointment to see him so she could explain her request. "We're arranging our wedding ceremony to bring together all segments of our past. You were an important part of the Hodgkin's era, but I can't imagine you in a bridesmaid's outfit. Would you provide an orchid for my bridal bouquet? It will be a beautiful symbol of hope and of your tender loving care." He eagerly invited her to see his orchids and agreed to bring one to the church on her wedding day.

Delaney walked down the aisle proudly carrying a spectacular bouquet of five white orchids that her oncologist had delivered that morning.

Causes

Through articles and lectures,
through conversations and media,
we hear that
   a lot of forces can be contributing factors,
   among the causes of cancer:
      stress   loss   heredity
        grief   depression   environment
      diet   pain   injury   atmosphere
        worry   neglect   habits
All of these are damaging.

Help us help our society
   deal with all cancer-causing forces
      so that the big enemy
        will not be fed
          by our neglect,
        our mistakes.

Medicine

This medicine we take,
we hope it
    will poison this monster in us, and
    not kill us off.

We need drugs with explosive power—
    to destroy,
    to reject the enemy invader.

But we hope it won't
blow us up!

Surgeon's Practice Disrupted

Her mother died of breast cancer when Mildred was a teenager. Deep in her heart, she felt that she would someday repeat her mother's story. By the time she was twenty years old, she was having yearly mammograms and was very careful about cancer prevention.

Her interest in health matters, her hard work, and her bright mind enabled her to become a surgeon before she was twenty-six years old. She loved her profession. She gave her patients and their families close attention. She also dreamed of becoming a wife and mother. She was married briefly to a man regarded by her friends and family as no match for her drive and her warm, loving personality. She was divorced several months before their daughter was born.

Close friends marveled that she was not resentful. She weathered the crisis well. She found delight in motherhood and in being a successful single professional woman with a thriving medical practice in pediatric surgery.

Four years later, "Mr. Right swept me off my feet," she said. After a romantic courtship, she found new marital happiness. "After we were married, he encouraged me in my practice. With his two boys and my daughter, whom he adored and adopted, we welcomed another child into our blended family. The baby sister arrived a year later. The blend includes the two of us with our four youngsters—his two, my daughter, and our daughter. We were living happily ever after, until cancer struck."

Her diagnosis was metastatic lung cancer. She was stunned! The monster she dreaded had crept into her life by another route. She knew that chemotherapy for lung cancer could have side effects that would damage her ability to do surgery. The prescribed treatments required that she take a lengthy leave of absence from her practice.

Sure enough, after an operation to remove a lobe of her lung and after months of chemotherapy and radiation, she was left with neuropathy—numbness in her feet and hands. The shock at not being able to continue her profession as a surgeon was as devastating as having cancer. She asked, "How can I reshape my life? I have everything I've always wanted—a loving husband and a beautiful family. Now the other huge part of my personhood, my profession, has been taken away."

To all outside appearances, Mildred was back to healthy, normal life—except that she could not do surgery. She had learned to walk, even to drive. She had learned to be conscious of her hands when caring for her small children and when she was cooking or driving. She did not endanger herself or anyone else.

She continued to study extensively in her professional field. She attended professional pediatric seminars and workshops. She was a successful speaker and based her presentations not only on her medical expertise but also on issues related to cancer and the professional woman. After two years, she officially closed her practice.

She kept a small office in her home and secretly wondered what the future could be. She worked to find new ways to be fulfilled as a physician. She and her husband could expect twenty more years together before retiring.

Laura's Messages

In twenty-seven years of fighting cancer, Laura had breast surgery twice and a hysterectomy. She announced that she would not have any more operations.

When cancer attacked her liver, she had chemotherapy.

Then metastases to the lung and skull required radiation and further chemotherapy.

On three occasions, doctors warned her, "It's time to get your affairs in order."

Each time, she replied with a saucy, "You're not the one giving life!"

One doctor insisted, "But you're terminal!"

Her prompt answer, this time in a gentle but firm tone, "I thought we all were."

A Visitor's Prayer

LORD, YOU have passed along to me
    a sample of YOUR concern for the sick,
    a gift I don't quite know how to use.
This person has a disease that terrifies me.
I don't want to be terrified—
    or to appear terrified—
    while I'm visiting.
Let me be composed,
    so I can embody YOUR concern.
I want
    to do it right,
    to say it right,
    to be the right person
        for these moments,
            for YOU and for
            for this person.
Help me be
    hopeful without being foolish,
    cheerful without being giddy,

> helpful without taking over,
> attentive without being nosey,
> concerned without faking it,
> constructive without snatching away anyone's
>   independence.

And, if it's not too much to ask, I would like
    both for this cancer survivor
    and for me
        to feel, later, that our visit was worthwhile.

With high hopes, Amen.

Alice's Arrangements

Alice was a single parent with two teenage sons when she had breast cancer surgery. Six years later, as the boys were finishing college, she married Mark and felt that her dream of a happy, normal, fulfilled life had come true. Mark, a widower, was aware of her health history, but it did not discourage him. Cancer had caused the death of his first wife.

Soon after Mark and Alice married, she had a recurrence. The disease had moved into other organs. Together they decided to make life as rich as possible. And while she took the needed treatments, she didn't let cancer dominate their life together or damage the ties they were building into their union, ties that included Mark's son and daughter.

In the spring before the graduation of her older son John, Alice needed an operation. She told her oncologist, "Okay. Let's get the surgery over with. But I will not miss John's commencement exercises."

The following year, her son Justin was to be married. By this time, Alice found that the tumor in her liver was enlarged. Her abdomen was noticeably swollen. She informed the doctors that she could not have surgery until after the wedding. "As I was selecting a proper dress for the mother of the groom, the saleswoman brought out dresses that were not flattering to my new enlarged figure. When I protested that I needed a more maternal style, the saleswoman replied, 'Surely your baby will be delivered before the wedding date!'"

Bonnie's Communication

Bonnie was proud of her communication skills, personally and professionally. She was in the hospital repeatedly. Each time, she was frustrated that she couldn't converse with her doctor.

He was business-like and thorough. He was competent and kind in examining her. The man was crisp and quick about giving her reports and explaining them carefully. However, in the hospital he usually talked with her from a distance, standing near the door of her room. He appeared suddenly, at odd times. She couldn't anticipate his arrival nor could she think of questions on the spur of the moment. Always preoccupied, he would depart abruptly, leaving before she could ask a question or even formulate one.

Alone, she scribbled a long list of questions on a pad, ready for his next visit. She thought, "I can keep them on the pad but not at the front of my mind or on the tip of my tongue."

Her inspired plan came during a sleepless night. When the physician arrived the next day, she put the plan into effect. She spoke in a faint whisper. Looking concerned and puzzled, he walked over to the bed and leaned over to hear what she was saying. Bonnie reached out, seized his belt, and held on. With the other hand, she reached under her pillow for the memo pad.

With her hand locked to his waist, she raised her voice. "Now, Buster, I have questions to ask, and I'll not let go until I get some answers!"

Jane's Rebellion

Jane was glad to be treated in the famous cancer center, but she was beginning to be annoyed. She encountered the notion that the model patient always must be quiet, cooperative, and pleasant.

"From my earlier experience in surgery and from extensive counseling, I had also learned that when you are ill, your emotional stamina is limited. You can't afford to put energy into pretending, to act like you have feelings that are not real."

On her way to surgery, with her husband walking beside her, she was wheeled into an elevator where "Nurse Authority" greeted them. Jane managed a slight smile. The nurse commended Jane, "That's good. We like to see good patients who are smiling and happy."

Her husband, Lewis, sensed that Jane was squelching the urge to growl. Her smile faded. She told him later, "I wanted to shout, 'What if you have to deal with me when I can't smile and pretend to be happy! Will I be treated as a naughty girl, a bad patient? What if I need to complain or shout about my pain?' I thought all that, but I managed not to say any of those things."

Later, in the recovery area, the nurse in charge warned Jane, "Your moaning and groaning disturb other patients. You need to be quiet, dear."

Jane thought, "I didn't know I was making any sounds. I wasn't aware that other patients are close by. I can't worry about them right now. My job is to hurt and wail. That nurse's job is to take care of us and to stay out of the way. She's not here to teach etiquette to surgery patients when we can't talk or complain. Never mind, I'm going back to sleep."

What's Normal?

One minute I'm feeling fine,
healthy and vigorous, cheerful;
    another, I'm sick, weak, and dreary.

Occasionally, I'm brave.
Sometimes, I'm panicky and cautious.

At the same moment,
I can be lonely-and-crowded,
    want to be left alone
    and want to be comforted.

When I am bold and trusting about the future,
I am also filled with doubt and fear.

Gracious GOD:

I've lost touch with what's normal.

For people dealing with cancer,
does everything have to be
    so important,
    so intense,
    so extreme,
    so full of risk and danger,
    uncertainty and worry?

Can we ever walk on level paths again?
"Maybe and maybe not" is not the answer I want.
Please, let me find normal.

Jessica's Demand

Jessica was no stranger to the cancer world. In fact, she was haunted by memories of two deaths—her husband's and her stepson's—each after lingering illness.

She had been retired several years when her breast cancer was discovered. She had a mastectomy and a swift recovery. At her final conference with the surgeon and a routine check-in with her family doctor, both told her, "Forget it. You're doing fine! The tumor is gone. You don't need treatment. There are no signs that you'll need further attention."

Jessica insisted that she wanted to talk with a cancer specialist. Despite her demands, both physicians refused to make the referral, saying that she didn't need that kind of help. She repeated her request several times. Both doctors consistently refused.

She had often described herself as a resourceful woman, "independent and sassy." She approached the local unit of the American Cancer Society and asked for a list of oncologists she could contact. She chose a woman, Dr. Laurin. In their first conference, the doctor talked with Jessica about her history and her worries, studied the records, and agreed to examine her regularly. Jessica liked her gentleness and her thoroughness. She asked to schedule visits every six months. The doctor expected Jessica to be a member of her own healing team. They agreed that they didn't want cancer to sneak up on her.

Nine months after the breast surgery, in a routine examination, Dr. Laurin discovered a tumor in Jessica's colon. She recommended a surgeon to have it removed, and she supervised chemotherapy follow-up treatments.

Jessica was glad to have Dr. Laurin as her teammate, ally, and friend.

Checkup Time

Time for a checkup!
I don't like the psychic straining and stretching I feel.
I'm tied in knots, pulled tight.

I want to be treated with dignity and respect.
If I have to be touched or probed, I want it done with
     gentleness.

I want to be calm.
I want to get good reports.
I want improved help and attitudes.
I want relief from pain and worry.
I want good news.
I want to be healthy.

If I get bad news,
I want to be tough enough to take it,

If this checkup brings me to a turning point,
I want to be flexible and determined
in the next phase I enter.

I want it detected if it's there.
I want to make good use of all the knowledge and skills,
all the equipment and medicine.
I want full reports from complete testing and thorough exams.

I want these forces to work for my benefit—
    YOUR love,
    the physical and emotional treatments,
    the powerful medications,
    my mental attitudes and my body's strength,
    my prayers,
the prayers and concern of other people.

Research, a Personal Litany

GOD, YOU are in the business of revealing truth to and
through human beings.
**Work in and through people and institutions engaged in
research.**
Rush up discoveries of the causes of cancer.
**Work in and through people and institutions engaged in
research.**
Show them how to prevent this disease that harms YOUR
children.
**Work in and through people and institutions engaged in
research.**
Help them devise procedures, medicines, and treatments that
will cure cancer.
**Work in and through people and institutions engaged in
research.**
Stimulate generosity in governments and foundations and
contributors.

Work in and through people and institutions engaged in research.
Please fix it so that I can benefit from this research.
Work in and through people and institutions engaged in research.
I want that cure!
Work in and through people and institutions engaged in research.
Please!

An Oncologist's Sense of Loss

Ruby was having her regular checkup with her oncologist, Dr. Scott. He examined her and reviewed her records, along with reports from recent tests. All the news was good. He asked her to schedule her next appointment for six months later.

When Ruby realized that the conference was coming to a close, she mentioned her friendship with Effie, a former patient of Dr. Scott's. "I haven't seen you since Effie's funeral. Maybe you didn't know that Effie and I were close friends. We met after each of us had been diagnosed. I'm still hurting over losing her. She appreciated you and your care. It must be awfully hard for you to lose a patient in whom you invested so much and for whom you cared so deeply over so long a period of time."

She was embarrassed when she noticed tears in his eyes. For a moment, he couldn't speak. Ruby felt that if he had tried to speak, he would have lost his composure. Visibly moved, he said after a long pause, "Thank you for mentioning that. I was very fond of Effie. I admire the way she fought her disease to the very end." After another silence, he added, "This conversation is the first time anyone has ever asked about my feelings as a physician caring for people."

As she departed, Ruby wondered how an oncologist with a heart full of caring could keep confronting death so frequently in his work. Then she realized that a heart—big and strong—is necessary for anyone working in this field. She also wondered if either his personality or his education had equipped him for handling such burdens.

Heal the Healers

GOD of healing, comfort, and encouragement:
Work through the healers—
    doctors, nurses, therapists,
    pharmacists, counselors,
    helpers (with bedpans and mops).
Work through them with power,
    with tenderness,
    with brightness.
Steady their hands.
Teach them that healers can also love their patients,
    without owning or controlling them.
Work in the healing team
    while they deal with difficult situations and difficult
        people,
    while they feel frustration and failure, disappointment
        and grief,
    while they cannot work miracles,
    while they balance their private and personal needs
        with the needs of people they help.
Comfort and encourage them with success,
    with visions of serving YOU and healing people,
    with invigorating companionship,
    with high and humble regard
        for the sacredness of their work.
Spirit of healing and Source of health, Origin of all life:
Live fully in the lives of people
    whose work is in the healing of others.

Baker's Medical Team

It had been hazardous investigative work, but Baker was putting the whole picture together. From his position as a long-term patient, he was figuring out the system, the network of physicians, administrators, therapists, nurses, technicians, researchers. He was finding out how they were arranged to fix his condition and, incidentally, run the institution. As a sociology and psychology major, he was putting all his sensitivity and all of his observation skills into action. With a patient's distinctive point of view, he wanted to unlock the mysteries of authority and monitor the chain of command that made things happen. The whole enterprise became his major therapy. Things were happening to him and around him!

He told his wife, Lolita, that he asked questions about the uniforms and insignia and what they all meant. "Badges and pins on the uniforms of nurses announce which are the big nurses and which are the little ones. Yesterday, a bunch of bags were hanging on this tree beside my bed, ready to spill their contents into my bloodstream. As I was lying here, staring up at them, I read the labels aloud. I read my own name each time it showed on a bag, 'Baker Mills, Baker Mills, Baker Mills, Margot Smith, Baker Mills! Wait a minute!' I started shouting and punched the button for a nurse. 'Margot Smith! Who the hell is Margot Smith? I'm not Margot Smith! I don't want her drugs dumped into my blood vessels!'

"The big nurse on duty, with little nurses trailing close behind, jumped to attention and rushed in here and took Margot's medicine away. They soothed me by telling me that Margot and I are on the same pharmaceutical protocols anyway. 'No harm done,' they cooed to reassure me."

That same night, in what he called "The Loneliness," he elaborated on his fresh findings. His reflection brought a new, important realization. "I must be part of the team as I move ahead toward a bone marrow transplant or stem cell replacement." A "Big Doctor" was pushing the marrow transplant, but another "Big Doctor" was recommending the simpler procedure.

Baker's wife and parents were more confused than he was. And they were more easily alarmed when things didn't go smoothly. Baker decided that he would have to be a responsible member of the team, with big doctors and nurses, therapists who had to be in his future. The team was to include nurses large and small, along with family and friends and anyone who wanted to pray for him.

His late-night musing continued. What would be his first step in establishing this team and occupying his place of responsibility in the network? He decided to use his research to clear up matters that had been bothering him. He was dealing with a number of noted authorities in specialized fields. There were things he wanted to know. How did all these people and forces fit together? Who monitors the connections? How do they communicate among themselves? Who gets to vote? How do they come to joint decisions about his treatment? Who could and would pull all the information together and interpret it to him and Lolita? When there were questions, and there would be many, whom should he ask? How could he double-check his medications and keep track of his scans and tests and records? How and when could he get chances or make chances to ask these questions? What decisions would *he* have to make? How much time would he have to decide? What benefits would come from any pattern of treatment? If he was unconscious or didn't feel like carrying his load, who would take care of all these duties?

When this period of reflection and planning was over, he wondered how to announce that he was ready to be a major player on this healing team. He thought, "Maybe I should get Lolita to bring me a crown to wear to show my authority— or a baseball cap with 'Coach' in big gold letters."

By morning, he was ready not only to take his medicine but also to issue some commands—firmly, but gently. He wondered how a big nurse or a strong physician would react.

He wondered if his sense of humor could hold and if he had enough nerve to borrow, from a big shot in his office, a desk sign that read "Boss." He wondered whether he wanted to wear the label.

Cancer Survivors' Findings

As a cancer survivor, I need an oncologist who can help patients regain dignity, recover control, seize hope, devour medical information.

When the doctor-patient relationship is working well, we trust each other. The patient can ask or say anything, no matter how absurd, to the doctor. The doctor listens and asks questions. Then the doctor evaluates and summarizes the evidence and explains the whole situation. The doctor also trusts the patient to reveal what happens, to tell about both feelings and facts.

From time to time, others work and play roles on my healing team—family members and friends, among others. They join the team with or without being invited. Whether aware or not, they risk bungling the healing process. With or without being aware, they contribute to the healing process. Many others show up for long-term and short-term involvement—neighbors, counselors, clergy, therapists, associates from the workplace, other healthy minded survivors, workers of all kinds.

Hope is one of the strongest medicines. Long-term hope is confidence that everything will be right eventually. Short-term hope is having something specific to look forward to. Doses of laughter also help.

The healing process works better if the people involved love one another. The team learns to work and play together without a lot of meetings or practice sessions, but time together is an essential component in the healing.

Because cancer is a shrewd, sneaky enemy, both the cancer survivor and the doctors stay alert, practicing surveillance forever.

Chapter 5

Strengthening Spiritual Stamina

"I needed surgery, rehabilitation, and radiation treatments. I also needed to get my inner self together, my soul nourished, my spiritual nature strengthened. I still do."

"The scientists are proving that prayer helps people heal, even when they don't know that others are praying for them. Without being aware of that research, I was counting on prayers from people I don't know, from people who don't know me."

"But this stuff is mysterious and unpredictable— cancer and its causes, treatments and recovery. So is health—mystifying. The spiritual dimensions of the cancer experience open up other mysteries. AWE-SOME! These mysteries are not to be solved but to be investigated, to be enjoyed and appreciated."

Lollie's Great Year

Lollie, a young widow, said, "I wish all my friends could have known my husband. Adam was a creative, carefree man, even when he was sick.

"After his cancer diagnosis, through the year before his death, he continued to make light of his situation. He laughed at himself and his ailments. When he was warm, even in a public restaurant, he'd take off his wig and brashly fan himself with it. As you can imagine, this often caused a scene, but he enjoyed showing off that way."

Lollie and Adam had always been close. Their marriage was important to both of them. They worked together as designers. They grew even closer during that final year of his life. Their son Adam was only four. Lollie knew that their time together as a family would be brief, so they were careful to make the most of it.

"I wouldn't have missed a moment of that year," she said. "We packed a lot of living into a short time. In some ways, it was the best year of our marriage, the best year of my life."

The Public

LORD, when will people ever learn about cancer . . .
    that the disease is chronic—not always fatal?
    that the disease is not contagious?
    that cancer patients have feelings, aches, pains,
       passions, dreams?
    that the whole family is affected when cancer strikes?
    that we can talk about other things?
    that cancer patients need something other than pity?
We need
    attention and privacy,
    independence and support,
    realism and hope—
    like anyone else.

Where Does Help Come From?

GOD:
Often I get surprised.

I am able to take my treatment,
go to radiation,
work every day and

go home to my helpful loving family,
acting like this is all routine.

I know people are praying for me.
Could it be that my energy,
my meager courage,
my good attitude
are gifts from YOU?

Have all those prayers from other people
opened up good channels for YOUR Spirit
to get into me?

Help me to remember to help others,
starting now and continuing after I get well.
Amen.

Kate's Call for a Chaplain

When it was time for her treatment, Kate checked into the
hospital for several days. Over a year, this happened at three-
week or four-week intervals, depending on reports from
blood tests. Each time, the side effects were severe. Kate was
violently nauseated for two or three days. She notified her
family and friends that she didn't want anyone watching her
vomit. She issued strict orders that they were not to visit her
in the hospital.

She was becoming bald. She quickly purchased a wig,
coifed to match her own hair in color and style.

This time, she was admitted to an institution that was new
for her. A volunteer in the admissions office helped her get
located in her room and assisted as she unpacked her things.
Kate was glad to have someone to chat with, someone familiar with the institution. She asked the volunteer to stay while
she changed into a gown and robe. They talked while Kate
repaired her makeup and fixed her hair.

Then she leaned back against the pillows and—in her most relaxed and regal tones, exaggerating her European accent—announced to this new friend, "Now, darling, I want to talk with the chaplain."

As a gracious hostess, the volunteer apologized that the hospital had no chaplain. Surprised, Kate sat up, put her hands on her hips, and issued an ultimatum, "Well, by damn, truck one in here!"

A minister arrived within an hour.

A Question, about Simple Lifestyle

Cancer is complex!
Treatments are complicated!
Living with cancer is confusing!

So,
how can I live
the profound,
simple
life now?

At the same time
the world around us
is satisfied
with simplicities
and superficial solutions.

And smart people are hooked on
dumb slogans
that don't say
or solve
anything.

How am I to live?

By
grace!?

Yes!

Matthew's Clues

Matthew was talking with a colleague and several trainees about learning from the people they were trying to help. "You want to know what I've learned from my work with cancer patients? I've learned a lot that can help anyone live better, can help us all, with or without cancer.

"For instance, one cancer survivor said to me, 'You know how to get over a fence? First, you throw your heart over.'

"As I see it, people with cancer, the ones who are doing well, have several assets in common. They get good medical care. They have some people who love them. They sense that they're needed. All of them seem to have some reason for living, something they want to accomplish. They have religious resources. They're determined to get well, and they work hard at it. And they're able to live with uncertainty about the future.

"Some patients don't live even though they have all of these. But the patients I know who are doing well are patients who have at least these necessary ingredients for living.

"And cancer survivors aren't the only ones who need these. I need them too."

Ada's Reunions

Ada astonished her husband, her family, and her friends by the ways she dealt with her illness. She and Bill were told that she could expect to live only six months, but both of them were working to extend that limit. "She's taking her treatments like a trooper, after she thought about refusing them," said Bill. "No signs of panic at all. When she decided to see the process through, she regarded her normal continuing schedule as part of the prescribed medicine. And she deals with the medical process as a necessary grind, not a series of tortures. Before she started losing her hair, she bought a wig that matches her usual hairdo."

She made contact with important people from her past, renewing several neglected friendships. She engineered visits by her children and grandchildren so that the visits would overlap without wearing her out. The arrangement prevented an overload but kept life interesting for her and her guests. She lined up other relatives and close friends and planned times for them to be her houseguests, shaping the invitations so that some stayed a few days and others stayed a full week. Bill commented, "Ada has set up a big reunion on the installment plan."

She continued writing, using both her journal and her poetry to define, describe, and ventilate feelings, to sharpen her observations, and to record her reflections. "She's not showing the literary output to anyone yet, not even me," Bill reported. "Too private, I guess. But she let me know that she's written out some directions for her funeral service. Eventually I'll get all that, when I need it."

As time went on, she let Bill take over many of the household chores she had always treated as her turf. She seemed pleased and surprised, when—unassisted by her or anyone else—he prepared one of her favorite meals. But Bill was careful not to create the impression that he could comfortably get along without her.

Bill also observed, "It's interesting that she's staying in character in so many ways. She's putting a minimum of effort into tidying up. Her closet, her papers, her desk are still disaster areas. She doesn't bother to make them neat. But she's going strong, in her own way!"

Linda's Prayers

Her sister-in-law was bragging on her: "Linda, you're the kind of patient who endears yourself to the people around you—other patients, your neighbors and friends, your family. You love everyone, and they respond by loving you. You choose wonderful small gifts, carefully selected and colorful, to remember doctors and nurses on their birthdays. How do you do all this?"

A nurse in the oncologist's office offered, "Linda, I wish you and Buddy would call me at night when you need help. I'd be glad to spend the night in your condo anytime."

After several operations, each more serious than the previous one, Linda realized that her condition was deteriorating, that the disease was out of control. She was talking with her pastor, Kelly.

Kelly asked, "Linda, how do you want me to pray for you?"

She had never been asked that kind of question before. After a long silence, she said, "I want you to pray for me to get well, of course. I don't like being sick. I'm tired of it and I want it to end." Then she paused.

"That means I want to get rid of this awful disease—for me and for everyone else."

Another brief pause, then Linda said in measured cadence, "But, Kelly, if I can't get better, I don't want to keep living this way. Pray for me not to have a lot more of this to deal with—or for my family to deal with. We've all had enough."

After another moment of quiet togetherness, she continued. "Yes, those are the ways I want you to pray for me, for me to be relieved of this misery."

Mystery

Holy GOD, YOU are mysterious to us always.
Now that we are dealing with cancer,
our sense of mystery is amplified, magnified.

We don't understand this disease,
   its responses to treatment,
   its impact on the psyche, or
   its effect on the body.

We're living with uncertainties
    about the side effects of treatments,
    about the length of our lives,
    about the effect on future generations,
    about prolonged, degrading illness ahead,
    about sudden onslaughts,
    about creeping, secret invasions,
    about ambushes awaiting us.

Give us courage and help us turn to YOU,
    even when we are puzzled,
    angry, anxious, mystified.

A Miracle, Please

O GOD, Source of all-powerful Love:
what I need now is a miracle, please.

I've been taught—by YOU and others—
to ask for what I want and need.

I'm ready to cash in on YOUR ask-and-receive offer,
    on that "knock and it will open up" deal, and
    I've rounded up others to join me in this request.

So, if YOU have any extra miracles lying around,
I really would like to have one.
I would like the surprise,
and I would like to surprise
    the folks who think I'm already dead.

YOU know, and I've mentioned it repeatedly,
    that things are pretty rough here and now.
        Here and now, I need big-time help.

YOU may choose to do the monstrous zap on my ailments.
YOU may select people to work through;
YOU may use the magic called medicine, or
YOU may work some of our faulty prayers so that they trigger
    a dramatic cure,

YOU may fix me—and all the rest of us—
   so we can endure and prosper,
   so we can cope and be whole,
   so we can put up with what we can't change,
   so we can do some good although we are ill.

Whatever! It's YOU and me, YOU and all of us
   together in this mess
   and in the VICTORY
      over our problems,
      even staring death in the face.

Ready! Let's keep going!

Becky's Chief

Becky, a hospital chaplain and a cancer survivor, shared her thoughts about her chaplain supervisor with a frustrated patient. She called him "Chief" in the privacy of her mind. Becky heard herself saying, "He can't deal with me except as a dependent, helpless cancer *victim*." Becky knew that a part of his problem was that he was worried about his dying mother.

Becky stated, "I'm very much alive, and I want to be treated like a living, productive partner. I don't want to be treated like a sick, wilted person."

"Yes, that's the trouble I'm having," said the patient.

Becky recalled another incident. "Chief was offended when I refused his offer to drive me to the clinic for my chemo drip. I didn't need that much help. And if I had wanted and needed help, I wouldn't want Chief to be the one to give it.

"Last week, he and I were walking down the hall together. He knew that I'd had a treatment the day before. He wanted to know if I was feeling all right, if I could get through the day. I assured him that I could handle my responsibilities. Then he blurted out, 'You confuse me! How long are you going to be around here?' I've got to put up with him while he's convinced I'm dying!"

Later, Becky had regrets about unloading her feelings. It wasn't professional to burden her emotions on anyone looking to her for care.

But maybe the patient will learn something from Becky's experience. She thought, "I wonder if I have the nerve to write up this interview as a report, to get the message through to 'The Big Chief.' Should I do it? I don't think so. I've already confessed and evaluated this incident."

Feeling Burdened

O GOD!
Life is so heavy now. When can I relax?

Everything is
so intense,
    of ultimate importance,
    significant in shaping the future,
    loaded with meaning.

Everything is weighted with meanings:
    a drop in the white count,
    a doctor not answering questions,
    a headache or a sprained toe,
    a hangnail or a bad hair day,
    or any number of whatevers.

Now I'm wondering if I'll ever understand what's happening
    to me.

But thanks for being here, GOD.
I count on YOU to care.
I've been leaning on you all along,
    so I intend to trust YOUR help as we move ahead,
    through and beyond my troubles.

I guess I needed to say that I'm troubled and overburdened.
I need and want
the sense of security YOU can give.

Cole's Motivation

The university medical center staff advised Ms. Ashcraft, the new medical social worker, to get acquainted with long-term patient Cole. She was told that he had unusual views of the cancer system and was eager for his experience to benefit other people.

Having studied his records, she approached him carefully. She did not want to force him to review his painful history as they were getting acquainted.

She asked cautiously, "What keeps you going through such a long and painful war with cancer?"

"Years ago, I was fortunate to be looked after by a pioneer in treating my version of cancer. It's rare, and the treatment options were more limited than they are now. Dr. Cunningham had access to the latest developments in research. Soon after my diagnosis, he and I formed a partnership that has lasted fifteen years, through one of the earliest bone marrow transplants with prolonged isolation, through several clinical trials for chemo. Now, we are considering a third BMT.

"Now I'm too old, and my brother's the only compatible donor available. I may not have the strength to get through it. At best, without it, I don't have long to live. So we're falling back on our original commitment in this partnership. I'm willing to do anything that may help research before I die. My family understands this 'mission' I'm on, though they're not enthusiastic about further misery for me. I don't have any other mission that I can take on at this point in my life.

"Now, dear new friend, I'm extremely tired, so we need to terminate this conversation. I've talked too much. And I've probably told you gruesome things you didn't need to know. But we can talk another day, okay?"

Ms. Ashcraft left Cole's room weary and sad, but wiser and encouraged.

Lynn's Baptism

At thirty-five, Lynn was diagnosed with lymphoma. Before her baptism service, she recalled the previous three years as a time of intense growth and prolonged pain. Lynn recalled, "The diagnosis almost destroyed me. Not the disease or the treatments but the realization that cancer had attacked and invaded my body was more than I could stand."

She remembered the people who had helped her get through that period. Her divorced parents reentered her life. Other supportive people were her friends and fellow cancer survivors Jerry and Rebecca. They had introduced her to CanCare, which gave her an opportunity to talk about and reflect on her experience. However, six months later, a drastic reoccurrence of the cancer jolted her sense of progress.

While hospitalized, she became involved in the church, initially through Kent, a minister who worked with CanCare. She discovered the church's troop of clowns. She hoped to join the group, but the bad turn in her health stole her opportunity.

Restricted and weakened by her condition, she stood shakily, watching for the arrival of Kent and the others who were to participate in her baptism.

She reviewed her spiritual journey. Always aware that God cared for her in a personal way, she never had felt the need to be officially connected with a church. She thought, "I've been surrounded by cancer survivors and church members who are like an expanded family I never had. Today, I'm becoming a member of that family."

Lynn was charmed to see people getting out of cars in clown garb.

Kent presided over the service, inviting Lynn to express her faith in God and conducting a brief Communion service.

On cue at the end, the clowns suddenly distributed red balls, fake noses for all to wear. After Kent's benediction, "Nothing can separate us from the love of God," there was a glad and loud "Amen" from grinning faces with red noses. As the group were leaving, someone commented, "This was a solemn and holy and amusing moment. I'm glad I was in on it."

After the guests were gone, Lynn said to her mother, "I don't know how soon I will die, but I'll be ready. I'm also ready to continue living with cancer. I expect to find the strength I need for each day. And I feel confident that God will take care of all of us forever."

Cancer Survivors' Findings

Prayers carry words, emotions, questions, requests, affirmations. In contact with God, openness is necessary, far more important than our words and phrases or positions or patterns. However, there is nonverbal praying—moaning and wailing, sighing and begging, stunned silence or holy laughter. All of these are elements in our spiritual linkage with God the great Healer.

Comfort, encouragement, strength, wisdom, serenity, joy, endurance, patience, determination—all of these are by-products of prayer, gifts from the One to whom we address our prayers. No formula can guarantee specific results. Prayer is its own satisfaction.

Questions haunt cancer survivors: Why me? Why anyone? Why does God . . . ? Why doesn't God . . . ? What am I to do? How can I endure? What's next? What does it all mean? Questions are more numerous than answers. Many answers raise new questions, and only a few satisfy. Questions are necessary, valuable, unavoidable, a way to understanding. Honesty is essential.

Mystery—reality beyond our understanding—shapes our spirituality, our connection with God. An evidence of this mystery is the human companionship that fires up our spirits. In other words, people with whom we are bonded are often gifts from God. Another dimension of this mystery is the fact that God chooses to be intimately connected with people who are hurting or damaged, who are being healed.

Chapter 6

Anticipating the End

> *"Cancer does not kill as many people as heart disease. Even so, many enlightened people think that cancer equals death. A lot of people treat us as though we are dying."*
>
> *"I hope to be doing something useful all the way to the end of my life. I want to live until I die."*
>
> *"God has taken good care of me, provided me with a good life, and given me toughness when life wasn't so good. I trust God to take care of me at the end and beyond. I don't need to know a lot of details about 'The Beyond.'"*

Here and Now

GOD of all times and places:

YOU live in the human scene, not aloof from it.
In our miseries and in our glorious moments,
YOU share our lives.

When pain produces loneliness,
    YOU feel that pain and
    YOU stay with us.

When we cry out,
    YOU cry with us, and
    YOU listen to our cries.

When we are weak,
    YOU move in, supplying YOUR power.
When we give up,
    YOU give us what we need.

When fear of death seizes us,
    YOU lend us YOUR experienced strength;
    YOU have been through it, and
    YOU go through that horror again with us,
        so we're never alone.

When a life gets abbreviated, cut short, unfinished,
    YOU show us eternal meanings
    crammed into brief periods of time.

When we stand at a graveside,
    YOU raise our spirits to new life, promise us
        resurrection,
    and breathe new life into our slouching frames.

And YOU are always inviting us to live YOUR
        kind of life
    HERE AND NOW.

Eunice's View of Death

Six weeks after Eunice and her daughters were told that she had inoperable brain cancer, they were talking about the memories they shared and about their future.

The medical news was not promising; in fact, they were told that Eunice might live only two months. Eunice's rare and deadly form of brain cancer showed up suddenly, diagnosed after she complained about moments of pain and confusion.

Eunice and her grown daughters were making the most of their time together. Repeatedly, they expressed thanks for giving and receiving good care in the current crisis and all through their lives. They spoke of happy times and they talked about difficult events. They reviewed spiritual resources that had shaped their family's life through the years, motivating them to love and serve people. One of the daughters observed, "These times were like family prayers or Sunday school in our childhood."

Occasionally, Eunice carried the conversation into diffi-cult territory. She brought up the subject of her approaching death. "I want us to talk about my dying."

Her daughters kept their composure, tearfully nodding to encourage her to go on.

She assured them, "I'm not afraid of death, and I don't want you to pray for me to keep on living." One of her admirable qualities was her well-informed faith. They had often drawn inspiration from her.

She continued, "I view the dying process the way I view my birth. I arrived here in this world without having to worry about leaving a comfortable place or about moving out into the unknown. I was delivered from one world to another, held in loving hands and received into loving arms, well cared for all the way. I had nothing to do with it. I expect the same as I'm moved into my next life."

Margaret's Choice

At seventy-six, Margaret had exploratory abdominal surgery. She was told that her inoperable cancer was widespread. The doctor explained, "Inoperable, but maybe curable, certainly treatable." She was not convinced by his encouraging demeanor.

Quietly but firmly she refused chemotherapy. No one could convince her that the treatments could buy anything more than a brief amount of time, and not quality time at that.

"I've looked after several relatives who had the misfortune of living past the age of ninety. I don't want to repeat their history. I don't want to be one of them. I've had my allotted three score years and ten, plus a few extra good ones."

She talked about another friend, an experienced hiker. She described him as "a person who rushes past a lot of pleasant stopping places."

Margaret said that she didn't want to go past any more pleasant stopping places. This was to be the one for her.

Bertram and Anita's Anniversary

It was the morning of Bertram and Anita's wedding anniversary. On the phone, Anita spoke with a neighbor.

"I don't understand what's happening here. You know how sick Bertram's been and how depressed—for so long! And today he's a different man. He's been looking forward to this weekend, but I don't know what to make of the changes in him this morning.

"You know how hard he's worked, trying to take his twenty pills a day. He's been throwing them up and losing any food he tries to swallow. He hasn't been able to breathe without the oxygen tube in his nose. The doctors haven't given him much hope of living very long.

"Four of the children and their families arrived yesterday for the big celebration this weekend. He could hardly talk to them. We could see that he's glad they're here. The other three kids are due to arrive today, for the reception tonight. The priest will be here and we're going to reenact our wedding. Several of our original attendants will be here too, so it'll be quite an event!"

It was amazing! Bertram got on his feet that morning. He announced that he didn't need the oxygen, that he wasn't going to take his pills, and that he wanted breakfast. She didn't know how to react. She wondered if he would make it to church the next day, and she worried that he might collapse at any moment.

He lived to enjoy the celebration. Anita said, "I'm seeing glimpses of the Bertram I married, a happy husband and

father, the life of the party, not the sick man we've been looking after."

The next day, Bertram was taken to the hospital, where he
died peacefully.

Staying Alive!

Almighty GOD:
Though this life doesn't go on forever,
    it is precious to YOU and to me.
We human beings are feeble and fragile,
    but we matter to YOU and to one another.

My dream is that
I'll always be surrounded by people
    who will let me make decisions.
Help me stay in the mainstream.
In other words, I want to live till I must die.
I want to be treated with respect, to be a partner in my own
    care.
There are things I don't want to happen:
I don't want people talking about me outside the door.
I don't want decisions made unless I have a voice in them.
I don't want to lose privileges and faculties—
    dignity, conscience, reasoning, enthusiasm, concern,
    humor, judgment.
I don't want to die inch by inch.
It's awful to dread losing parts of my body,
    organs or limbs or whatever.
It's terrible to fear the loss of my senses—
    hearing, seeing, touching, tasting, smelling.

Protect me from useless worry,
    keep me focused on each day's brightness,
    help me find ways to live through grotesque times,
    and build into me determination to find causes for
        delight.
Please enable me to make the most of all my days.

Cooper's Finale

Cooper had begun to settle into his bonus years. "My gold watch is now almost five years old—the one they gave me when I retired," he said. "Now I'm enjoying time with my wife and our only daughter.

"What have I given up? I'm no longer handling records for our employees' credit union. As always, our social life centers in the church, and we're part of an old timers' crew at the cafeteria every Tuesday evening."

Soon after this conversation, Cooper learned that he had cancer. After surgery and a series of radiation treatments, he was labeled "in remission." He moved back into normal activities. When asked about Cooper's cancer, his wife bragged, "He was a good patient and I was a good nurse, but we're glad that's in the past."

Two years later, his life became more complicated. Additional surgery and follow-up treatments left him weak and sad. Family and friends were attentive as his health faded. One friend remarked, "We all enjoy visiting with him, and he's interested in what's happening. But his illness has him pretty much locked into the house. It's hard to see him going downhill now."

Cooper, sensing that his wife and daughter were exhausted, insisted that the doctor contact a hospice agency. A hospice nurse scheduled an "intake interview" in their home and was planning to arrange in-home service. Suspecting that he was weakening fast, she took his pulse and blood pressure. She instructed Cooper's daughter to call for an ambulance. As she continued to care for him, he became still and drifted into unconsciousness. The nurse said quietly, "We won't be needing the ambulance after all. I'll cancel that order and contact the funeral home for you while you say your good-byes. Assume that he can hear you. I'll stay with you while we make the necessary arrangements and phone calls."

Haunted!

HOLY SPIRIT:
I'm occasionally asked,
"How do you live so well on the edge of life?"
My usual answer goes something like this,
"What other choices do I have?"

YOU and I know that
tomorrow things could change and
life would be shattered and I would be dead.

I'm grateful that today
we—YOU and I—are defying the odds.

I'm enjoying every minute.

Please,
keep those minutes coming.

Uncle Ike's Perspective

As a lifelong friend of Bruce and Nell, Isaac didn't feel that
he was intruding on a private family conference when the
doctor spoke with the family about a serious development in
Nell's cancer. The family was crowded into a small conference room. Bruce and Nell's son Judson had a firm grip on
the arm of "Uncle Ike."

The physician summarized Nell's situation and prepared
the family for the next era. The message seemed cruel, but his
tone was gentle and kind. Ike listened carefully, knowing that
he might be called on to recall details of this conversation.

The doctor explained, "You have to realize that what
you'll be seeing from now on is not your wife or mother, not
your sister. What you'll see instead is the power of the disease as it takes complete possession of a person."

Ike wondered if it was necessary to draw such drastic pictures. However, he realized that the physician was helping
them understand Nell's disease. Ike was sure that their emotional distress would not make them abandon her. She would

get their love and tender touch. She would still need them till the end. The doctor's message was telling them to toughen up. He was also helping them find a different perspective, unpleasant but necessary. Isaac needed it too, as he intended to stay close with them and with Nell through her final weeks or months.

The doctor went on, "You need some time, while she's recovering from this operation, to make some plans. But before you get too busy or before you become too worried, give yourself room to absorb the reports from today. Talk all this over, and we'll confer when you're ready. I'm available anytime you need me or anytime she needs me."

Prayer, at the End of Life

GOD of peace and comfort:
All these people around me are
    grieving, telling me how much they will miss me.
That's comforting, but I need another kind of comforting.

They are getting ready for their loss, as they "lose me."
At the same time, I'm getting ready to lose all of them
    and everything else I love or care about.
I can assure them that I'm okay about dying, but
    I can't comfort them more than that.
I don't expect them to comfort me,
    and I don't know that I can find comfort on my own.
I'm facing immense unknowns,
    and no one goes with me when I go.

It's not the ultimate future I'm worried about;
I trust YOU to take care of that, as I've said before and often.
It's the immediate nonphysical pain of parting.
The time of departing stretches from days into weeks.
The time of leaving everything that's familiar and dear to me
    is long and dreary, especially when I'm alone.

It's hard to enjoy each day
    when this cloud is hanging over it.

I do have reasons to be glad and grateful—
    creature comforts, rich memories, and noble companions,
      among others.
Help me focus on these and find others
    so the days and nights will be brighter and I can feel
      better.

More and Better Life

O GOD, Giver of life:
Life has been good,
    in spite of cancer.
I didn't ask for it.
I didn't want it.
But I'm grateful
    for what I know now
    and for what I am now
      that I could never have known,
      never have been
      otherwise.
Now I want to build on
    this base.
With YOUR help,
    I want to preserve what I've been given,
    and I want to keep growing.
Please,
    I would like for this new life to keep going.

Annie Clyde's Retreat

"After the news I had from the doctor yesterday—and after all these years of good and bad health because of cancer—it's time for me to go on a retreat for the good of my soul. I want to tidy it up before I get so sick I can't think clearly. Thanks for endorsing my plan to have Barbara go along. Several days on our mountain will do me a world of good." Annie Clyde was checking signals with her husband after the disastrous news that she could not expect to recover, that the cancer had invaded vital organs. Further medication could be effective in controlling pain but not in reducing the tumors.

Annie Clyde wanted the retreat for spiritual nourishment, but she also wanted to give her husband a break from his around-the-clock alert. If she went to the lake, he could catch up on his other responsibilities. Barbara, a registered nurse, could manage the pain medication and move effectively if a medical crisis should occur. The two women were not sisters, but they had grown up in the same household and had looked after each other and each other's children.

While confronting the last weeks of her life, Annie Clyde could talk with Barbara about accomplishments she was proud of. Barbara had always shared the satisfaction that came from Annie Clyde's civic activities. Barbara also shared her interest in spiritual disciplines. As they drove to the cabin, they talked about how to use the retreat time. Annie Clyde said, "I need to claim a large slice of time for private meditation and prayer and Bible reading. I won't be studying so hard this time. I'll be feeding on what I read. I expect the Psalms to be my main course for comfort and encouragement. I've always wanted to do my own exploration of the emotional expressions—ugly emotions as well as beautiful ones—in that Old Testament poetry. Those writers 'let it all hang out,' as the kids used to say."

Barbara chimed in, "Let's use our snack and meal times for remembering good and tough times we've been through. Maybe we can crow over how great we've been and about the good we've done and the good times we've had. If you feel like it, we can stroll through the woods, but I don't want you straining yourself to prove that you are still going strong. It's time to admit that you've fought the good battles and are now claiming the right to retire from the fray."

The precious days and evenings unfolded pleasantly. Annie Clyde found new serenity. One evening, she suggested that they fantasize about the future careers of each of their children. The two mothers drew verbal pictures of their grown offspring twenty years in the future. They predicted each as highly successful in their chosen fields. They sketched all of them, together and separately, having to endure the same devilment they had inflicted on their mothers.

Both of the women had grown up in the church, so they used its rich phrases for morning prayers together and for separate, private meditation. They compared experiences of prayer and inspiration at each stage in their lives, and they talked about the values each had found in imagery as well as conventional prayer-words. And, of course, they talked at great length about the impact of Annie Clyde's cancer experience on both of them and on their families.

Barbara was fascinated with Annie Clyde's use of the Psalms. She explained, "At this stage in my life, I'm looking for words, phrases, ideas that fortify me for this final illness. I've marked all over this modern translation. At points, I write my own name where the writer says 'I' or 'me.' Then I change pronouns from 'he,' 'his,' 'him' to 'she,' 'her,' 'hers' so I can be sure it fits me as a woman being liberated. I've also marked words loaded with emotions, especially emotions I've felt in my battle with cancer. There's a lot of anger—angry complaints about the way things are—in the Psalms. And there's joy and peace and there's fighting spirit and high hopes. I need all of that!"

She thumbed through to a favorite passage, Psalm 8, and read her rephrasing of that poem:

> O Lord, our Lord,
> Your greatness is seen in all the world!
> Your praise . . . is sung by children and babies . . . .
> When I look at the sky, which you made,
> at the moon and the stars . . .
> What is woman, that you pay attention to her;
> mere woman, that you care for her?
> Yet you made her inferior only to yourself;

You crowned her with glory and honor . . . .
O Lord, our Lord,
Your greatness is seen in all the world!

After a quiet moment, she added, "I think I'll have that psalm as one of the readings at my memorial service. See to it for me, when the time comes."

Mrs. Allen's Support

The widow Mrs. Allen called the village where she lived "Tinytown, U.S.A.," and she loved it. She called the whole population "my extended family," especially after her husband died. They had no children, so all the parents taught their children to call them Uncle and Aunt.

The whole village went into shock when her cancer was diagnosed. They wondered where they could turn for strength in times of crisis.

When she became ill, she wondered who would help her deal with her illness. Her new pastor had been there only a few months. It was his first parish, and he lived ten miles away. To his surprise, Mrs. Allen unloaded on him the details of her Stage 4 cancer. Her tears flowed as she told him about the long days in the cancer center. She could see the young minister crumbling before her eyes.

She sat up straight and declared, "Young man, you are my pastor! I need you to pray with me. I need to be honest with someone if I am to get through this horrible experience, so you will have to be strong enough to help me. Now I'm tired and sick. I need someone to lean on."

She saw him straighten up in his chair. He spoke in a clear strong voice. "Mrs. Allen, you can count on me. I'll need to learn from you about this disease and how I can help. You can count on my visits and my prayers. You can call me anytime, day or night."

He visited her regularly. The best help came in the form of his prayers with her. He didn't know whether he helped. He knew she had helped him stretch, to become the person and the pastor he wanted to be.

Someone to Listen

Ever-present GOD:
All these people, and no one to talk with.
No one can hear how good or how bad I feel.
No one can really share my horrible thoughts,
    help carry my heavy burdens.
I don't really feel like shifting my load
    to someone else's shoulders.
They cut off comments when I need to talk
    about uncomfortable topics.
They tell me I don't need to feel that way or
    that things are not as bad as they seem
    or as dangerous as they appear to me.
They say I'm fretting over things that may never happen.
So I'm left with my pain
    and my fears
    without external support,
        except YOURS.
Hold on to me, especially when I can't hold all this in.
Thanks for letting me know that I can count on YOU.

Eugenia's Graduation

Thelma insisted on providing lunch to celebrate Eugenia's release from hospice. "I'm inviting myself to lunch with you at your home, and I'm bringing the lunch. We need a celebration. I never heard of anyone leaving hospice before. Are you their first graduate?"

At lunch Thelma reminisced, "We thought the breast surgery would be the end of the fight. Little did we know!"

"Yes," said Eugenia, "I was thrilled when the doctors said that all I had to worry about was some lymph gland involvement. Radiation was supposed to take care of that."

Thelma continued, "I remember thinking that you couldn't have made it without your strong determination, your faith and optimism, and that amazing hopeful attitude of yours.

"I was there a few months later, during a regular checkup with the oncologist. He told you that your disease had spread to your whole skeletal system and that there were tumors in your lungs and lymph system."

"His words have haunted me ever since," Eugenia said softly.

"A month ago, you were getting weaker by the day. The doctor said it was time for you to move to hospice care. Your husband Royce took a leave of absence from his work so he could be with you as much as possible."

"Royce tells me I slept most of the first week. The thing I remember is being sick. Royce was there all the time, except when he came home to check on things and to get fresh clothes."

"Now, tell me how you got out."

"There's not a lot to tell. The staff said goodbye as we walked out to the car. I'm glad hospice is available if and when I need it again. I graduated.

"After that first week, I began to feel better. My vital signs improved, and my appetite began to pick up, and I was getting stronger each day. I wanted to come home, and the doctor was glad to dismiss me. I feel safe at home now. Can you believe that God is giving me another chance to live? I may be the first graduate from hospice. And next week, I'll take you out for lunch. Another celebration! My treat next time."

Complaints and Questions

GOD!
I can't stop wondering why this happened to me,
    why it happens to anyone.

What lessons are we to learn?
Lessons of patience and determination?
    I could have learned them another way.

Lessons of humility and smallness,
    my mortality and my weakness?
    I could have been convinced without the torture.

What benefits come to me from these circumstances?
    They could have been delivered another way.

Can it help anyone else for me to go through this?
    I'm not convinced.

GOD?

A Mother's Christmas Story

Our thirteen-year-old son Walter designed and produced the Christmas celebration for our family, and he was thoroughly enjoying the results of his work. So were we, his parents and his brother and sisters. My husband, Joe, and Walter and I had decided in August that this was a good way for Walter to use his strength and mental abilities through the weeks after his brush with death. He was excited about planning the best Christmas his brother and sisters could ever have.

As they opened gifts and squealed at the surprises, he saw his success. Cuddled beside me, his fatigue was showing, wrapped in pleasure.

He was tired not only from his work on our Christmas celebration; he was also worn-out from the illness, from the efforts not to be a burden to anyone, and from trying to act as mature as possible in these distressing times.

August had brought physical disaster, almost death. For three nights, the nurses and Joe and I were all convinced that Walter couldn't last another twenty-four hours. His mind was clear and he was able to communicate. He talked with us, thanked us for the care we had given him through the years, and commended the quality of our parenting. He put his thin arms around us and assured us that he was ready to die, that he was convinced he was going to be better off after his death. He hoped that we wouldn't have to be sad about his dying. About this time, Joe told someone, "Walter is a very mature, intelligent young man. He's entitled to know everything that's going on. We talked with him about his beliefs regarding life and death. He has lived his twelve years fully and well. He's made valuable contributions to medicine and to his family. He's had the strength and faith and nerve to say, 'I'm going to die first, to show you and my friends how to do it. I'll be there waiting for you.' He has an unfaltering trust, confidence, and faith in the steady care of God."

After the three-day crisis, Walter rallied. In the middle of September, he told his parents and the hospital staff that he wanted to go home. Doctors told us that hardly any blood was getting to his brain. They couldn't understand how he was staying alive. After returning home, he began to take exercises, to eat nutritious meals, and to play bridge. He didn't attempt to go to school or to take courses with the teacher who worked with homebound students. Without fanfare, he gave his personal treasures to his brother and sisters.

Joe, Walter, and I decided that he was to work on the family's Christmas celebration. He studied mail-order catalogs and circulars from department stores, figured costs, placed orders, and arranged the budget. He was enthusiastic about the plans and was glad to work on them. He was happy about arranging the happy event for all of us.

When December rolled around, Walter couldn't take solid food. The tumor was blocking his esophagus. He had difficulty swallowing. He was losing weight steadily; he looked "bony." He could sip soup now and then, and he could eat a little ice cream. We wondered whether he could last until Christmas.

On Christmas morning, Walter asked to be carried downstairs before the others so that he could watch their faces when they saw their presents under the tree. From my lap, he viewed the scene eagerly as they opened the gifts. He used his full strength to hold his head up. As the festivities quieted down, he let his head rest on my shoulder. I wondered, as I held him, whether he would ever be able to raise his head again.

Grief

GOD, help all these people—
Help us—deal with this loss.
I wasn't close to this person
    but I feel the loss.

We shared the basic experience of this damned disease.
We shared more than a common enemy, though.
    We both felt pains—our own and each other's.
    We both dreamed that we could defeat this enemy.

It's not fair!
It's not pleasant!
YOU know that!
I know that!
This patient knew that!

Use my feelings for this comrade in the war.
Use these feelings to heal broken hearts.
Use these feelings to develop fighting spirits.
Use these feelings to strike blows against the enemy.
Use these feelings to make life better for all the rest of us.

Use the pains I feel,
    to make me more sensitive and more resilient.

Take my sense that the world has been robbed
   and transform that sense
   into determination,
      so I can invest in the world YOU love.

M. C. Mosely's Final Weeks

The foursome gathered for a lunchtime visit because of their devotion to and admiration for M. C. Mosely, their friend, neighbor, colleague, and mother. Angel, her business associate and successor, had invited the other three to update her on her mentor's condition. It became an occasion for leisurely reminiscing. M. C.'s daughter, Elvira, explained to their hostess, "Angel, you haven't met Debbie the hospice worker who's staying with Mother. She doesn't think it's proper to call an older woman by her initials. And she surely wouldn't call her 'Mary' or 'Mary Compton,' so Mother has been addressed as 'Mrs. Mosely' more often in these last two weeks than she has in several years."

Alex and Maria Campbell had lived next door for thirty years. Alex commented, "Debbie's been great. She called us a couple of times and apologized unnecessarily each time."

Elvira responded, "That was true until Mother had that setback three weeks ago, and we both knew we couldn't handle it unless we had outside help around the clock. The doctor had explained that hospice would be the right solution. And hospice has been, with all the expertise and experience, the sensitivity and wisdom. They keep precise records, they brought in handy equipment, and they've coached Mom and me about what's going on, what's coming next. The nurse gets here in a hurry when we need her. The whole staff and the volunteers have been attentive. I can go to my room and sleep at night, knowing that I'll be called if I'm needed. Now I don't have to stay alert or stay in the room with her through the night. With a clear conscience, I can go off in the daytime to look after my clients."

Angel, who had bought M. C.'s business at her retirement, said, "This is good news to me—not that she's so sick but that she's getting superb care from you folks who have been close to her through the years and from the hospice system. Now that it's too late, I wish I had told her again how much I appreciate her as a friend and admire her as a role model for a lot of us women who entered the business world at midlife or later. She encouraged me to take a bold new direction when I joined her staff. She started this enterprise after she turned sixty-five, while your dad was so ill—with his encouragement, I understand. Did he know he was dying then?"

"Oh, sure! They both knew he couldn't recover. Everybody knew that at the time," Elvira volunteered.

Maria mentioned, "You weren't living here then, and both of your brothers were established with their families on opposite sides of the country. Your dad wanted M. C. to have a constructive outlet for her energy and to have something to occupy her mind after he died."

Angel observed, "A lot of people, including me, benefited from working with her. She built a business that served international firms dealing with relocation issues. And on the side, she was a champion networking person for women like me in the men's world. But she played that role without animosity toward or from men. She was amazing!"

Alex interrupted, "Through the church, after her retirement, she helped us retirees make the most of our later years. She told us she had decided to concentrate on volunteering, but she didn't want to distribute recycled clothes to the needy or teach children in the Sunday school again. Someone else could do those things. Our group of old-timers has been a roaring success, with a New Year's Eve gala that's been the talk of the town. She told us she'd decided to concentrate on her church and on her alma mater, as a faithful alum with organizational ability. And she did both in fine style."

Maria giggled, "A funny thing happened in all that. The church was looking for someone to look after arrangements when a death occurred, to care for the family and all the ceremonial procedures. She told them quickly that she didn't want to be the 'Death Lady.'"

Elvira recalled, "When her cancer was getting the upper hand, she was still working on her college's celebration—for alums and board members and faculty and students—the 150th anniversary of the founding of the school. She was accumulating an impressive list of dignitaries and celebrities to enhance the national event. She made arrangements for her cochair to take over. A few days ago, the president of the college called to inquire about her and to send good wishes."

Maria chimed in, "She did move in powerful circles. It's so sad to see her reduced to such a frail, fragile creature. She can't communicate except by giving yes or no signals when she's asked a question. And she can do that only in brief moments of consciousness."

Alex took over again, "It's amazing that after she was sixty-five she built that business. Since her cancer surgery, she's done all that work for her college and all that work for us seniors. And now, I guess she's finishing the course, showing us how to live victoriously all the way to the end."

Elvira said, "Mother's sense of humor has never failed her, even in these last months on the downhill course. Angel, did you hear about her planning with our pastor for her memorial service? They laughed and wept their way through all the details. She had strong preferences. He called them 'fixed ideas,' but he liked most of them, and they argued over some of the features. She asked if the congregation could sing the 'Hallelujah' chorus at the close of the celebration. He felt that there were other ways to close on a joyful, triumphant note. They compromised on a rousing Easter hymn as the recessional. They chose scripture passages to be read, and they agreed on a level of simplicity, personal components, and other concerns.

"Somewhere along the way, he made a smart remark about wanting her to help design his funeral if he died before she did. He pointed out that their plans depended on her dying before his retirement at the end of the year. Otherwise, she would have to rework the plans again, with his successor. She made a quick comment, 'And wouldn't it be funny if I goofed by not dying!' "

Cancer Survivors' Findings

Loved ones, as well as pastors, priests, and rabbis, want to be available, present, and helpful. Their presence and wisdom can provide personal and pastoral attention—strengthening and soothing when death approaches.

Cancer forces us to think about death and dying. This warning is both a curse and a blessing. It is an unwelcome distraction while we need to put the emphasis on living. It is a blessing because the cancer survivor is prompted to think through how to spend the last chapters of life. We are given time to say our good-byes, to think constructively, and to plan for the dying process, including the services after death.

Although our society leads us to hide the inevitable, all of us die. We don't like to confront our mortality. However, the final moments can be rich, packed with memorable meanings for all.

The dying process need not be gruesome, alarming, confusing, or degrading. Hospice, the medical profession, and other agencies can protect us and our families by means of pain control, by interpreting the progress of the disease, and by anticipating the next steps.

Chapter 7

Tasting the Victory

"You asked, 'When and why do you celebrate?' Here are a few answers. I remember celebrating on many occasions: When I could do ordinary things again, like clean or cook or shop or go back to work. When I swallowed a pill and didn't throw up. When my hair grew back. When the doctor said, 'The next appointment can be in three months instead of one.' When I went on a short trip out of town, an outing. When I got a good report. When an anniversary rolled around. When I saw my children go through high school graduation."

"Is it possible to have full life and fun after cancer? Yes!"

Gray's Golfing

When cancer was discovered in his right leg, Gray was told that his leg had to be amputated. He was given a choice: Doctors could either remove the whole leg or save a six-inch stump of the upper leg. He said he could think of no constructive use for the salvaged stump, so he took the doctors' suggestion. The whole limb was removed, all the way to the hip socket.

No one told him that he couldn't play golf again. But he guessed that was to be his fate. He was distressed that golf had to become a thing in his past.

In his rehabilitation, the prosthesis caused pain and pressure up into his torso. He migrated to soft, upholstered seats. With the prosthesis, which he named "Rick," he decided to try a round of golf. Rick didn't cooperate. If the terrain was uneven, Rick kept him from making a full, good swing and from maintaining his balance. Of course, much terrain on a golf course is uneven.

However, Gray recalled that the therapists had been impressed by his steady stance when he was on one foot, before Rick joined him. So Gray decided to try out his game without Rick. He used only crutches, a golf cart, and his good leg. It worked! It was great!

After several weeks, Gray had again become a regular fixture on the golf course, with his one-legged game and a reasonably good score. He was pleased with this development—until the sight of him caused an accident. One morning, while teeing off, he heard a loud crash behind him. Wheeling around, he saw an embarrassed woman climbing out of a wrecked golf cart. She had crashed into a tree while staring at him. She was upset that she was caught staring at the crippled man. Gray tried to soothe her, but he couldn't squelch a chuckle.

Another time, a foursome came up behind Gray and his buddies and were waiting to tee off. They watched as Gray moved to the ball for his second shot. Aware of the audience, he hoped to get the ball to the green and make it look easy. His swing was smooth, and he watched the ball bounce respectably onto the green. He thought of turning to take a bow for the group behind him, but he resisted that urge. Gray was striding ahead on his crutches when his partners signaled that he should look back at the tee. Each golfer there was standing on one foot, with his other heel in the air, practicing his drive from the stance they had seen Gray take.

Gray commented, "I don't recommend this as a way of becoming a celebrity, but I enjoy it when it happens!"

Decisions! Tasks! Decisions!

Oh, GOD, I'm counting on YOU to be generous.
I need a lot of help in a lot of ways.
At this point in my life as a cancer survivor, I need to
   adopt some attitudes
   do some weeping
   have some laughs
   set some limits
   gather some information
   fix some goals
   arrange some priorities
   make some plans
   remember some medical terms
   face some facts
   adjust some values
   encounter some harsh realities
   learn some coping skills
   get some rest
   utter some prayers
   discover some meanings
   arrange some diversions
   weather some conditions
   cool some anxious friends
   calm some relatives
   make some changes
   gather some good thoughts
   take some nourishment
   endure some tests
   see some doctors
   swallow some medicine
   think some thoughts
   raise some questions
   hear some success stories
   find some options
   drop some bothers
   make some complaints
   accept some waiting

    tolerate some treatments
    trust some people
    locate some helpful partners
    make some plans
    select someone to talk with

It's hard work, dealing with all of this, so I need help deciding. And I need help doing. I'm counting on YOU!
Help, please!

Betty Ann's Body Parts

As a new member, Betty Ann thought she might shock the cancer support group by introducing herself this way, but she hoped they could take it. They were cancer survivors too, with a few professionals along for the ride. She chose the bold approach.

"Three years ago, I had a mastectomy. Three months later, the other breast had to be removed. Since then, I've had reconstruction, so I have two new boobs." A couple of soft gasps were heard from the group, but no one flinched at that point, so she continued.

"Last year, I had cataract surgery on both eyes, with lens implants. Very successful!

"A few months ago, I broke both wrists in a fall while I was playing tennis. I now have matching pins in my arms. I got rid of the slings last week.

"Bit by bit, I'm becoming a bionic woman, but I've had enough. I can't think of anything else I want to do bilaterally."

The group's laughter welcomed her.

Shawn's Two New Lumps

When he was fifteen, Shawn developed Hodgkin's disease. After going through painful treatment, he recovered. As a recruit for CanCare, he went through a strenuous training period. By listening and by offering friendship, he was prepared to help others with cancer—especially other young persons—deal with their morale problems. Through this organization, he also received invitations to speak to several civic clubs. He enjoyed telling adults in the community about his experience with cancer and his work with several younger survivors.

The summer after his seventeenth birthday, Shawn noticed two lumps on his neck near his right shoulder. The doctor said that the lumps would have to be biopsied. If the tests showed a malignancy, he would have further surgery and repeat his earlier treatments. His mother and father were frantic. They hated to think about Shawn going back through those difficult months. They were afraid it would be more serious the second time. His mother said, "He's approaching his senior year in high school and he has a lot to lose, not to mention the pain and the anxiety for him and for all of us."

His parents were concerned that Shawn didn't seem at all bothered. They couldn't imagine that he was as "cool" as he appeared. They thought he should show some panic, to react the way they were reacting, to admit that he was alarmed. Finally, both of them insisted that he sit down and tell them how he was feeling. They assured him of their love and promised to stick with him whatever happened.

His response was, "Mom and Dad, you two don't understand. I've been through training about cancer and about my feelings. I've learned that 80 percent of all lumps are benign. If these two turn out to be malignant, there's something that can be done about it. Look! The treatments worked before. If I have to go through it all again, I will. But I don't have any reason to get upset until we hear from the lab tests."

His mother called to say, "Shawn may not appreciate it fully, but his father and I are grateful to you at CanCare for its training program and for your effect on our young man. Whether you ever change the world of cancer survivors, you helped our family survive a trauma. We thank you!"

What If?

Okay, GOD, what if . . .
 I get cured?
 a recurrence grabs me?
 my health skids into a ditch?
 I run out of money?
 I die suddenly, or gradually?
 I lose control of my body, my mind, my situation?
 my family and friends can't take any more?
 they desert me?
 the doctors say there's nothing more to be done?

It will all be up to YOU and me, then. Right?
I'm glad YOU and I are in this together.

I count on our being together always.
I'm grateful not to be alone.

Lori and Eric's Toast

Lori was a prominent socialite in her late fifties. She had never told friends that, in the early stages of their marriage, she and Eric had named her breasts Gloria and Pattie.

The afternoon before her mastectomy, she was weeping quietly about the loss when Eric entered her hospital room with a bottle of wine. He brought out two glasses and grinned, "Let's drink a toast to the friend we have both known and loved."

"Okay," she said, "let's drink to Gloria."

"To hell with Gloria," her husband replied. "Let's drink to Pattie. She's staying with us."

Lori's giggle replaced her tears.

Carrie's Mislocated Breast

Carrie had wondered whether anything funny ever happened in the cancer world. When it did happen, the joke was on her.

"Displeased with several versions of breast prostheses," she said, "I invested a bundle for a valuable, beautiful boob. I wore it proudly and comfortably. No dangers, no disasters! Then I went to the beach with my brother and his family, and I lost it!

"I was swimming alone, though family members were fairly close, enjoying the sun. I was careful about staying in view of the reunion group on the sand. When I realized that my big investment was gone, I was standing in water up to my neck. With a hand where my prosthesis should have been, I was exploring the bottom of the ocean with my toes and crying like a baby!

"My brother noticed that something was amiss. I was moving around cautiously. He rushed out to see what was happening. By the time he reached me, I was frantic. He embraced me and asked, 'Why the tears?'

"I sobbed, 'I've lost my new, expensive boob! How will I ever find it on the bottom of the ocean?' I wailed.

"He pulled away from me and, pointing at my middle, burst into laughter. He said, 'Either we've found it or you've grown a new boob where your navel should be.'

"My tears of distress were replaced by hysterics of relief."

Thanks

Thank YOU, God . . .

for YOUR care delivered in human beings: doctors, nurses, therapists, pharmacists, receptionists, technicians, clerks, aides, housekeepers, social workers, volunteers, families, friends, visitors, researchers, counselors, pastors, other patients;

for YOUR power working through things: medicines, food, drugs, sheets, pillows, gowns, x-rays, scans, needles, probes, swabs, lotions, water, tubes, pitchers, cups, phones, television, radios, bottles, trays, pills, lotions, bandages, machines, carts, computers, charts, records, thermometers, bedpans, drips;

for YOUR soothing touch: through words, handclasps, pats, hugs, embraces, caresses, baths, massages;

for YOUR commands and challenges: Exercise! Diet! Fast! Breathe! Stretch! Schedule! Stand! Sit! Lie! Turn! Twist! Bend! Stoop! Step! Stop! Go! Reach! Relax! Grasp! Hold! Wake! Sleep!

for YOUR reassurance and encouragement: in notes and cards, casseroles and visits, tears and diversions, flowers and nods, music and silence, convictions and promises, happy faces and solemn warnings, laughter and smiles, sunlit days and moonlit nights, darkness and sparkling stars, bright dawns and cleansing rain, films and books, solitude and companionship.

Thanks a lot!

Amanda's Revenge

Amanda made a hit in her CanCare survivors' training group when she told them her outlandish tale about putting one doctor in his place.

She told about a routine checkup with her gynecologist soon after her breast surgery. The opportunity came while he was taking tissue for her Pap test.

She reported, "I had a chance to get even with all male doctors. I was the voice of all females at that moment. I was on that table for the Pap smear, with my feet in the stirrups and my knees in the air, robbed of all dignity. While I was in that awful position and the doctor was probing for the tissue he needed, I lifted the sheet and looked him in the eye. That took him by surprise. Then I said, with mock innocent curiosity, 'Young man, does your mother know what you do for a living?'"

Laughter roared, loud and long. Several laughed until they were in tears. A moment of triumph for all!

Two days later, one of Amanda's timid classmates said to her quietly, "I want to thank you. My introduction to cancer came three years ago. When you told your story about the gynecologist, I realized that I hadn't had a good belly laugh in three years. Thank you."

Emma's Skin

When Emma was diagnosed with breast cancer, she was quite young—in her early thirties, a wife and the mother of three children, ages two, four, and seven. She could remember the date; it was her ninth wedding anniversary.

After surgery, months of chemotherapy and radiation followed.

She had barely finished that course when the oncologist reported that ultrasound tests revealed a mass on her ovary. It was likely to be malignant.

Fortunately, surgery and tests revealed that it was benign.

Four months later, she was diagnosed with colon cancer and had surgery to remove a large portion of her colon and uterus. It was her tenth wedding anniversary.

Two months later, shortly before Christmas, she found a lump in her other breast. A biopsy showed that lump to be benign, but the workup showed multiple suspicious microcalcifications.

The following March, she had a double mastectomy, a pre-cautionary measure. The first two attempts at reconstruction failed, due to significant radiation damage to the skin across her chest. She had avoided the complex breast reconstruction because of the extensive, multiple abdominal surgeries she had been through.

When reconstruction became her only option, she was demoralized. "Eight surgeries, chemotherapy, radiation, and multiple procedures in a three-year period left me physically, mentally, and spiritually exhausted.

"My husband, best friend, and soul mate—all in one—had seen me through all these tough times. This man, who had fainted during childbirth classes, had learned to flush a nasogastric tube, empty bloody drainage lines, and help with dressings. As we faced this decision together, he turned to me, and with a generosity so sincere it brought tears to my eyes, told me that I had gone through enough. He would donate the skin I needed to reconstruct my breasts.

"After a tearful moment, I told him, 'I appreciate the offer. But the last thing I would want in a moment of passion is for you to reach inside my nightgown and find yourself caressing your own hairy chest.'"

She was able to provide her own tissue donation, but they continue to laugh together about his generous offer.

The Gift of Tenacity

Look, GOD:
We've heard the words and we've said them:
    Hang in there! Hold on!
We're weary of hearing it, tired of saying it.
And we're tired from trying to do it—whatever it is,
    hanging on, hanging in,

holding on, holding down, holding up,
holding out, holding back.

We've been holding up,
watching ourselves hold back from expressing ourselves.
We've been holding on to our dignity,
our self-respect, our convictions, our people.
We've been holding on to YOU.
We've been holding on to all these helpers.

So we know about holding on, holding back, holding, holding.

We've learned about tenacity, learned that we need it.
What we want is tenacity that brings energy,
energy that moves, marches, accomplishes,
stamina to finish plans, to bounce up when we're down.

We want and need tenacity that risks and dares,
that grasps new—even dangerous—options,
that invests in experimentation,
helping research find better treatments and basic causes
that can help others and may help us.

What we need is more than endurance.
What we are asking for is YOUR kind of tenacity,
the kind that does not give up on us human beings.

YOUR version comes with brains and heart, muscles and even
guts.

Lula's Award

"The man is an oncologist! But he's a physician of the soul
and a magician!" Lula was telling her neighbor Ruth about
her recent visit with Dr. Shaw. "He didn't have to figure out
that I was depressed. I told him so as soon as he stepped into
the examining room."

Ruth was her strong support through Lula's years of dealing with colon cancer. On request, Ruth could summarize
Lula's history. "It has messed her up and messed up most of

her body. The cancer may have met its match in Lula. She went through repeated surgeries, defied dreary predictions of approaching death, and endured strange patterns of chemotherapy. She returned to her work with preschool children after each incident, sometimes wearing a wig or a turban, and sometimes showing off what she called her 'crew cut by Mother Nature.'"

Lula continued the account of her recent visit with Dr. Shaw. "I reviewed my cancer history. I reminded him that I had recovered from the initial surgery after a few weeks and was able to get back to work quickly. Then I had the liver surgery—maybe the most dramatic treatment I've had—but the liver reconstituted itself soon. I had a harder time after the double surgery when it got to my lungs.

"Then I skipped to the brain surgery three months ago. I've been discouraged ever since I got out of the hospital this time. I seem to have used up all my spunk. I was dealing with big-time depression.

"This was a regular checkup following the brain surgery. I realize now that I needed to see him for morale reasons. He always boosts my spirit by telling me something interesting about his research or research he's heard about. And he always brags on me—how good I look—even when I know he's lying, or he tells me how much progress he sees on my charts.

"This time, I was so low that I couldn't be boosted up. I moaned about how sick I had been and how crummy I felt and how my husband, Arthur, must be worn-out from taking care of me and taking me all over the country for treatments. But Dr. Shaw wasn't going to leave me in that condition. First he said something like, 'You don't know how lucky you are.' I spat back at him, 'You call this lucky? All these operations and all these treatments and all this misery—physical and emotional—and you call me lucky. I don't think so!'

"Then the good doctor came on full force. He said that I was a hero in the war with cancer, that I was a veteran of several serious battles and had been able to survive in the worst of them. He said that if I had been in the military I would be wearing a chest full of medals and ribbons. With that, he pulled a handful of junk out of a pocket somewhere. I don't think it was in his white jacket. He poked around in this stuff and pulled out a small scrimshaw pendant on a string. It had a ship carved on it. See, I'm wearing the pendant! He said, 'You can get a chain for this later. We're going to have a ceremony and award you a medal. Nurse Craig, will you get her husband in here to witness the ceremony?' He left the examining room for a few minutes. When he came back, I had dried my tears and I was wondering what was going to happen next.

"He brought Arthur in, along with two or three other staff members from the office and one of the nurses I like. He made this elaborate speech about what a hero I was and how I had won all these battles with cancer. He said that it was time to give me a special award for bravery and determination and good spirits, for courage under fire. He declared me a wounded veteran in the war with cancer. He slipped the string over my head, hung the scrimshaw piece around my neck, and kissed me on both cheeks while the gang applauded and whistled. It must have disturbed the other doctors and patients, but that didn't bother him."

Ruth said, "I bet you were in tears again after all that attention and praise."

"I was. And I felt a lot better! Now the pendant's on this fine gold chain Arthur bought that same afternoon. Anyway, after I got dressed, when Arthur and I walked through the waiting room, all the folks cheered and applauded. Two of the men stood up and whistled. Someone shouted 'Congratulations!' Everyone waved, and I waved back like a celebrity in the Tournament of Roses parade. We left in smiles. He is a magician, I tell you."

"And you are heroic!" added Ruth.

Colleen's New Eye

"Kenneth will always be in public life. After he decided to run for State Attorney General, we found out that I had cancer in my left eye—melanoma. The campaign had barely started. He and I both wondered if he should withdraw from the campaign. We quickly decided that would be ridiculous. As an act of confidence in God and in the medical possibilities, we needed to go on with our life, to act as normal as possible."

Colleen was telling her story to a local newspaper interviewer several years later, as Kenneth was being encouraged to run for governor. To the journalist's request for details about the cancer experience, she replied, "Well, I don't mind telling the story. I don't publicize it, but when someone asks, I'm glad to tell a success story, since there are so many sad stories out there about 'cancer patients' and 'cancer victims.' I'm glad to speak out as a healthy 'cancer survivor.'

"I was fortunate that the tumor in my eye was minute when my ophthalmologist found it. I had broken my glasses and had gone for an examination instead of having the prescription refilled. Very fortunate, right? At that time, the only sensible option was to have the eye removed, to get rid of the monster. Again, I was glad to find out that there was no evidence of spread within the eyeball or beyond.

"But I don't want to leave out some of the fun parts of the story. The artist who was to make my prosthesis—my 'glass eye,' as they used to say—was also very thorough. He had a hard time matching my eye color—not green and not gray and not blue, with odd flecks of other colors I had never noticed. He and I became good friends and were able to joke about the project before he finished. I wanted to order a whole set for different occasions—one for scowling at my children when they needed to be corrected, another that would glow glamorously for candlelight dinners with my husband, one that would look tired when I needed sympathy, a moist-looking one to wear to sentimental movies, and maybe a bloodshot version for the morning after a big party.

"Yes, we laughed our way through some of the alarming times. I didn't want my disease or the results to endanger Kenneth's political career. At one time, he said something about publicizing the fact that his wife is a one-eyed sorceress, but I didn't want anyone thinking that I'm into witchcraft, so let's keep that term off the record, please.

"As I was saying, we managed to laugh a lot, and we had some good help along the way. A neighbor and colleague of Kenneth's told me before the surgery that he would initiate me into the deformity club after my surgery. He has an obvious limp as a result of an accident in childhood, and his wife has had cancer. He was with Kenneth during my surgery and stayed until the physician reported that everything was okay. I didn't get to see him at the hospital. Before bedtime that evening, I called this couple to tell them that I was qualified for membership in their exclusive club. Later they told me that I deserved a special award for recovering quickly enough to make that phone call—only four hours after the operation.

"Then, on the day when the patch over my eye was removed and they began to fit the prosthesis, those two showed up with a certificate of membership in the Deformity Club International. They invented the certificate for the occasion—even had it lettered by a calligrapher. It hangs on a wall at home. It says that members are both deformed and deforming and so is society. That's not a political statement to be quoted. It was healing humor for me, but many people would be offended by this kind of foolishness. The paper, complete with a gold seal and signatures or forgeries, named some of the rights and privileges of members. I can remember some of the wording: 'infrequent seizures of self-pity; spontaneous outbursts of rage, giggling, weeping, praying; weird attitudes and philosophies; access to sisters and brothers who ail and help; steady or sudden surprising supplies of grace; occasional but convincing—even outrageous—experiences of victory over absurdity.'

"And the names on the document were ridiculous and encouraging. Apostle Paul's was in Greek, a blind friend signed in braille, another person who had lost an eye had signed. They also added so-called signatures of Helen Keller, George Washington (who had teeth made of wood), Van Gogh, Captain Hook, and Pinocchio. There was a footnote saying that mental quirks and strange attitudes do not qualify a candidate for membership. They pointed out that not all deformities are visible. We are not required to display our deformities in public.

"Sometimes I invite other people to sign my certificate, but I don't recruit members. I do recruit people to support Kenneth's campaign, so let's talk about that now."

Memories and Hopes

Thanks, GOD,
    that even in distress it is possible
    to remember happy moments—
        days, persons, events, occasions.

Thanks for helping us along rocky roads,
    over high barricades,
    through dark passages.

Thanks for glorious celebrations, quiet certainties.

We want protection from pain;
    but more than that, we want patience and strength;

but more than that, we need lively companionship;
but more than that, we can have confidence in YOUR
    love—
    the only gift that lasts forever.

In the days ahead, we need
    pleasant moments,
    calm spirits,
    open sharing, and
    vital hope.

Over the long haul,
    we will treasure the love we give and receive.

By YOUR grace, by YOUR power,
    our lives are rich and full.

Estelle's Dramatic Role

When Christopher was in his teens and his sister Cynthia was in elementary school, their sister Estelle was born. All four members of the family were delighted with Estelle. Each of her "four parents" showered affection on her, in happy rivalry for her attention.

When Chris was a senior in high school and Cynthia a middle school student, Estelle was moving out into the world by charming her kindergarten teachers and students.

Their world was shattered by news that Chris had leukemia. The diagnosis was slow and tedious, finally confirmed after weeks of tests and a longer period of feeling "rotten." Distressed that he was missing his graduation festivities and that his entry into college was in jeopardy, family and friends rallied to give moral support and to encourage him as he went through the treatments.

The disease went into remission promptly. He regained his health and entered college on schedule. A supporting throng gave him a glorious send-off.

During his college career, the disease returned with a vengeance. He was in grave danger. Specialists prescribed a bone marrow transplant to save his life. Family members and other volunteers were tested to find a suitable donor. Young Estelle insisted that she be tested along with the grown-ups. With everyone else, she wanted to help her idol, her big brother. Estelle was the only person who qualified. Another call went out for volunteers, but Estelle continued to insist that she wanted to be the one to give bone marrow for Chris. No other donors were found. Chris did not want her to go through the agony of the procedure, but she was determined.

Fast forward five years. Estelle became a teenager, Cynthia was in college, and Christopher had finished college and graduate school and was settled in his first full-time job. He was in love with Cynthia's college roommate, and they were planning to be married. Both fathers were clergymen, and they would conduct the ceremony in a favorite chapel in a mountain community where both families spent summer vacations. The bride chose Cynthia as her maid of honor. Chris chose as his chief attendant, "someone better than a best man. I want the one who saved my life and who made it possible for me to be here. I want my sister Estelle to be my best man."

Estelle responded, "Okay, if I don't have to wear a tux!"

Again, fast forward to the rehearsal dinner, a time for toasts to the bride and groom. Estelle gets to her feet. "Before saying my congratulations and best wishes, I have something else to say to my brother. You're welcome! My blood makes you look good. I'm glad I could help."

Anniversary

A strange event to celebrate, we know.
But it marked the beginning of a different life for us,
    so we mark the date each year
        as the days on the calendar creep along, crawl past.

LORD, YOU know we're glad to make it around
through the seasons again. Thanks!

YOU and we have been through a lot in the last twelve
months—
ups, downs, narrow escapes, disappointments,
conquests, worries, unexpected blows, unexpected joys,
touching moments.

YOU and we can be glad that a lot of that's over.
We can celebrate endurance and stubbornness.
We look forward with hope and joy and peace.

At any rate, we're ready for a fresh start into another year.
Let's not go back through the dreary pieces of the past.
Let's preserve the strength that developed through these past
months.
Let's carry forward the benefits we've gained.

Let's develop
in us patience,
human ties that can be mutually helpful,
inner resources and external props,
confidence for dealing with uncertainties,
victories to build up encouragement.

YOU hold the past, present, and future.
Hold us up as we move along.

Please.

Cancer Survivors' Findings

*God intends for us to have good life. It can be good even
in tough times. Often we have to fight to make it good.*

*When we deal with serious illness, it can be solemn and
dreary, but if we look carefully, we find it sprinkled with joy.
We battle pain and misery until signs of victory show up.*

*When dealing with life-threatening issues, we and our
families feed on gleeful moments, savor sentimental occasions, and delight in routines.*

For us cancer people, humor takes many forms. We have to laugh at our own awkwardness and mistakes. We can defy gruesome reality by the use of jokes or pranks. We ridicule procedures that put us in absurd positions. We use humor as an antidote to self-pity. We view harsh realities from weird angles, and we find that healthy-minded people "tell it like it is" to the tunes of comedy.

We cancer survivors have to live on the edge of life, haunted by uncertainty and possible terror. Pray for us to learn to live by using healthy diversions, sound judgment, holy stubbornness, creative strategies, and patient endurance.

Grateful for a second—or third—chance, we cancer survivors address our gratitude to God by reaching out to share our joy and by giving steady friendship to others who need encouragement.

We who have gone through the cancer experience find that opportunities to celebrate explode along the way. We can create ceremonies, reasons, and occasions to praise the One who does all the healing.

Chapter 8

Lois Ann Peckham
Tells Her Story

One Volunteer Speaks
for Many Cancer Survivors

I was honored and almost overwhelmed at invitations to speak about my experience with cancer. One invitation was from the Board of Directors for CanCare, others were from my groups of business and professional women. My college debate team experience, my years as a professor, and my career in banking have made me comfortable as a public speaker. In other words, I have learned not to panic before impressive audiences. Of course, I started off by thanking these groups for rescuing me during my crises, with practical help and moral support, and then I briefly told them my story.

Here's what I said: "I'm here today to tell you about my experience with cancer, but the first important thing is to say 'thank you' individually and collectively for your concern. You have given me power through your attention, your helpfulness, your gifts, your flowers, your visits, and your prayers. And the fantastic soups! I'm going to compile a soup cookbook for the very thin. We'll make millions! Because of their health problems, my parents were not able to be here when my cancer recurred, so it appeared that I would have to go it alone. But no! There you all were, committing your time to be on call and available, month after month, as I went through the chemotherapy rounds. At times, I was overwhelmed by this undeserved bounty. I don't have the capacity to express how very important your love and prayers have been and continue to be. You truly are conduits of God's love and grace in the ways you gave yourselves to me. I thank you with all that I am. I am still aiming to write a note to each of you.

"Nine years ago, I was diagnosed with breast cancer. Fortunately, no lymph nodes were involved. I had a modified radical mastectomy, but no radiation or chemotherapy was necessary. Since then, I have monitored my health very carefully. Two years ago, after a four-month effort to diagnose seemingly unrelated symptoms, the original breast cancer was discovered in my lungs and throughout my skeletal system. Metastases had happened to me in a big way! The doctors also found cranial nerve damage, most probably caused by the cancer. My right soft palate and my right vocal cord were paralyzed, so I could swallow only certain liquids. My speech was restricted to a hoarse, rasping whisper, not pleasant for me or for people trying to hear me.

"I made some careful decisions about my primary physician and about treatment facilities. I began what has turned out to be an eight-course treatment of chemotherapy. The cancer is still active, though greatly reduced, and it's located now only in certain areas of my spine, pelvic bones, and posterior ribs. The last two chemotherapy treatments didn't result in a reduction of the cancer—a development the doctors call "stabilization"—so I have been taken off the chemotherapy protocol for at least six months. I'm taking Tamoxifen, a hormone therapy, in pill form. My vocal cord is still paralyzed, but my ability to swallow has greatly improved and I can eat almost anything now. The general statistics for those with my type of metastasized cancer, treated with FAC chemotherapy, indicate that 80 percent will live less than five years and 20 percent will live more than five years. I will undergo tests every two to three months to determine the status of the cancer.

"In his correspondence with the Christians in Corinth, Paul the Apostle wrote, 'When the test comes, [God] will at the same time provide a way out, by enabling you to sustain it.' I had been in treatment several months when a good friend broke down and confided in me that one of her greatest fears was that if it happened to her, she wouldn't have the courage to deal with it. I tell you what I told her—you would! The promise to the Corinthians was that there's always a way out. We are not rescued—we are enabled. The 'way out' is the capacity to sustain, and the power of God is available to enable us. *To sustain* means to keep up, to endure, to keep from failing or giving way, to bear up, especially for a long time. *To enable* is to give power to, to strengthen, to make fit, to make adequate. When we are in deep and terrible pain or fear, we want it gone, and quickly. Too often that is not possible. Courage is the ability to function in the face of fear. God strengthens us, so that we can keep on going.

"CanCare volunteers and staff are channels of God's strength and love, enabling—giving power to—newly diagnosed cancer patients to sustain, to keep going, to endure. I know personally the invaluable gift of being loved by CanCare people, of being cheered, supported, educated, buoyed, empathized with, and filled with hope and faith. I also know personally the invaluable gift of giving that love and support when I serve as a CanCare volunteer. In his book, *How We Die,* Sherwin Nuland states that all the definitions of hope have one thing in common: They deal with the expectation of a good that is yet to be, a perception of a future condition in which a desired goal will be achieved, even in the face of terminal illness.

"I have chosen to rely heavily on conventional medicine. There is a reason why chemotherapy has the reputation it does, like most scenes of fierce battle. War causes a great deal of short-term and long-term damage beyond the actual battlefield. But in my case, my immune system was so overwhelmed that chemotherapy was essential. For instance, at one point, I nearly died from pneumonia. I didn't die, and I'm glad I decided to go with the program. I would probably not be alive today if I hadn't.

"However, I also rely on alternatives to conventional medicine. I meditate. I practice deep breathing. I work actively to reduce stress. I practice important visualizations I developed with the help of a hypnotherapist. I'm a believer in and practitioner of prudent herbal and vitamin therapies. I continue the psychoanalysis I began two years ago. Since I have regained some of my ability to eat, I'm modifying my diet in ways that boost my immune system. I work with a massage and reflexology therapist as often as I can.

"I'm learning to love my body, to integrate it as inseparable from my self, to see that I *am* my body. At the same time, I've relinquished at least some of my false vanity. Having a bad hair day takes on a whole new meaning when you have no hair!

"I consider the specific areas of my body that have been most directly affected by the cancer—my bones, my swallowing, my lungs, my voice, my spine—and I seek metaphors that I can use to contribute to my personal growth and psychological healing. How can I use the loss of my voice as a signal to be quiet and listen? How can I better nourish my soul? Am I disabled from a weak and damaged backbone? These are not idle or casual musings. They are avenues to personal growth that I would not have walked without the cancer.

"I honor important passages in this illness with rituals.

"I have spent more time in solitude than ever before in my life. It has been difficult, because I am so extraverted. And I have so many wonderful offers for companionship. I love people, all kinds of people, people of almost every imagining. When I am well, I get a lot of energy from others. However, at this time in my life, my spiritual and psychological healing—and to a large extent my physical healing—has made solitude essential for me. I have made and used the time to think, to write, to read, to pray, to sleep. As many of you know, I have had an insistent and deep desire for several years to have six months of time off. I wasn't expecting to get it this way (watch what you wish for!), but I consider it one of the most valuable gifts of this cancer experience. Believe me, I'm not the same person I was in May two years ago.

"Prayer has been and is the blanket around my life. It is the glue that holds me together. Prayer works and has healing power, whether the cancer kills me or not. I *know* that God is present with me. Science has tested and confirms, has validated the conviction that prayer heals—whether the one who prays is near or distant, is a believer or not, whether the one prayed for knows about the prayers or not. Prayer is love, connection, energy. It is the greatest gift you give to me and to others for whom you pray.

"I'm learning to live in the moment. Time for me is coming to mean this day and this day only. We all know it, ill or well, that this is the only way to live and the only time any of us has for sure. But for me, it took death moving into my house to begin experiencing this reality. In simplifying my life in this way, I'm much less likely to get overcommitted. I'm discovering that when you don't overcommit you are open to experience and open to savor the holy moments, to discover the deep joy that comes from the ordinary. I am more conscious of how I use this one day I've got. You can be assured that if you see me doing something now, it is evidence that I made a careful choice to do it, whatever it is.

"Maybe you wonder how I deal with the prospect of foreseeable death. I do not yet know if it will be my fate to die from the cancer, but it is appropriate to face that possibility, in case the disease does take me out. Death is inevitable for us all, though most of us don't feel the urge to think about it quite yet. I don't mean to suggest that I can always do it well. I often have times when I am extremely anxious and alarmed, but those are different feelings from being afraid to die. I don't want to die soon, and I fervently hope that I won't, but I'm not afraid. It's sort of like Woody Allen's famous line: 'I'm not afraid to die—I just don't want to be there when it happens.' Much of my anxiety centers around the process rather than about death itself, and around giving up this life rather than about facing or fearing the unknown.

"During these months of solitude, I've read and thought a great deal about death. I respect all thoughtful views of spiritual matters, of death, of life after death or no life after death, and my view of religious traditions makes room for them all. I would never suggest that my views should be yours, but I will share some of mine. As simplistic as it may seem, my personal view is that we as individuals have an encounter or encounters with God, or Yahweh, or a Higher Power, or the Divine One, or whatever your terminology may be. As a result of those encounters we are accountable for our own relationship with the Source or Great Mystery or Ground of Being. My personal religious tradition is Judeo-Christian. I'm an Episcopalian. During the past year, by the grace of God, I've come to *know* that God loves me, and that knowledge has given me the faith to accept the unexplainable, the mystery. My faith—that there is an 'other side' that is beyond all time and space and human imagination—is so strong that there are times when I'm filled with joyous anticipation. I passed a church billboard announcing the quote for the week the other day: 'Faith unemployed is peace unenjoyed.' My faith brings me peace. And my Southern Baptist heritage insists that I tell you it is available!

"Let me elaborate on this acceptance that comes from faith. I read from a page in my journal. These words were written several months after my recurrence, while I was in treatment. 'This cancer has enabled me to see that the surrender required of me is not about losing. Surrender is a process of acceptance. Accepting the reality of death—really accepting it. Accepting the promise of paradise. Accepting my scale and limitations. Accepting the irrelevance of power or lack of power. Accepting the inability to manipulate fate, and accepting the invitation to participate in my destiny. Accepting the divine in the ordinary. Accepting the challenge of becoming healed. Accepting the God within me. Accepting the gift of today. Accepting the love others extend to me. Accepting the truth, for the first time in my life, that God's name for me is my real name.'

"I'm beginning to know redemption. I know it in the waves of joy, of happiness, of serenity, of suffering, of grace. The cancer has called me out of the parking lot of my provisional life and into action. I am recording the holy moments and I am cleaning the attic.

"Now I want to talk about some philosophical terms—fate and faith, destiny and paradox. These terms have helped me make sense of my cancer experience, with all its mix of pain and victory.

"Physically and psychologically, I view having cancer as my fate. You might call it 'unavoidable circumstance.' I don't believe that I caused the cancer through anything I did or didn't do. I don't believe that God has punished or betrayed me. It is simply my fate. Living in God's world involves mystery and evil. God puts up with these miseries. God even endures them with and in us.

"How I carry that fate is my destiny, and that matter is very largely in my control. By carrying my fate correctly, even gracefully, I contribute to my becoming whole.

"Those two concepts form a paradox, and a paradox is a situation in which two seemingly opposite truths operate simultaneously and in the same location.

"For example, I echo the experiences of many when I say, very honestly, that the worst thing that ever happened to me is the best thing that ever happened to me. Another: The very thing that may kill me is the catalyst for my healing, for my becoming a whole person. In these past months, I have distilled my daily goal to holding in tension the paradox of two seemingly opposite objectives: On the one hand, I strive with all that I am to live; on the other hand, I am at peace with fore-seeable death.

"Those remarks take care of my need to share with you some of my philosophical pondering.

"As I understand—from my study and from my long musings in the glare of daylight and in the solemn silence of the night—the grace of God is the force that made us and that looks after us now and forever. That grace could not have been earned or designed by any one of us. It is God's eerie way of loving, even though we do not deserve it.

"I have talked about fate. God's grace enables us to face the harsh realities of our existence, the unpleasant and the unbelievable and the mysterious. God deals with these same realities; indeed, God is in this creation with us. As we face the harsh realities of human existence, we are not alone. We need honesty and realism as we encounter the gruesome side of life; faith opens the gate for God's grace to empower us to cope and conquer.

"But God's grace also takes the shape of hope, that equally eerie certainty that we can look forward with tenacity, discipline, and determination—knowing that eventually good will win out over evil, that there is always something ahead that will fill us with joy and peace. That high hope, future life, is painted in images of strutting around on golden streets, floating on puffy clouds while playing harps, resting from all arduous endeavors, wearing white robes and jeweled crowns. All of these images are imagination's way of saying that it will be better than anything we can imagine. The oppressed sing of freedom, the poor dream of riches, the weak of power. We sinners dream of being pure and even holy. Of course, the lame and the ailing look forward to good health and robust and vigorous living. Paul the Apostle insisted that God's people will be provided with 'spiritual bodies,' that we will rise up in a cosmic resurrection from the dead. Those are the long-term pictures that grow in the garden called hope. In the meantime, we have glorious experiences of finding new surprises—by God's grace—in our bouts with cancer, in our efforts to improve the world, in our spiritual growth, in our coping with life's problems. Hope gives us a vision to look forward to, a goal to work toward, a desirable future to anticipate. When I was in treatment, I hoped for at least a modicum of improvement. It was the vision of hope that enabled me to swallow my medicine or tolerate the side effects or find another goal.

"These gifts of grace—hope, faith, joy, and peace—are causes for celebrating. A ceremony that celebrates these gifts echoes through the CanCare Affirmation used at many of our gatherings. We recognize the harsh realities, we enumerate the tough times, we identify the struggles and the confidence, we embrace the faith, hope, and love that endure. CanCare uncovers hope for the cancer patient. Our mission is reflected in the CanCare message shouted as a litany at the end of meetings: 'Life is a gift! Let's celebrate!' "

A CanCare Affirmation

LIFE IS A GIFT! LET'S CELEBRATE!
We treasure life.
We have discovered how delicate we are,
how precious human beings can be.

We have found truths we did not want to know,
studied lessons we did not want to learn.

LIFE IS A GIFT! LET'S CELEBRATE!
We have confronted death,
have walked along precarious paths,
have fought back the dangers.
We have decided to live as long as possible,
and as fully as possible.

LIFE IS A GIFT! LET'S CELEBRATE!
We have experienced losses,
endured pains, faced limits.
We have found that we can cope—
claiming dignity and grace,
gaining help from others.

LIFE IS A GIFT! LET'S CELEBRATE!
We appreciate the connections with God
and with other human beings,
a complex network of holy ties
with healers and with unknown partners.
We receive strength through these connections—
energy to keep us going and
to make life worth living.

LIFE IS A GIFT! LET'S CELEBRATE!
We move ahead into new life,
carried by confident hope
into a doubt-filled future.
We are fortified by joy, armed for victory over difficulties,
even the threat of death.

LIFE IS A GIFT! LET'S CELEBRATE!
We intend to share
the power that has come in our pains,
the care that has held us up,
the life that we are given,
the faith, hope, and love that last.

LIFE IS A GIFT! LET'S CELEBRATE!

Afterword

How CanCare Works

> *"I was terrified and lonely. News that I had cancer triggered an avalanche, crushing me and destroying my dreams. The first time I heard of CanCare, nothing registered. Then someone asked if I would like a contact with someone who's been through what I was going through. Why not?"*

A person with cancer gets that kind of offer and opens up for a contact. A CanCare volunteer visits. The two share confidences, describe feelings and worries, compare experiences, admit weaknesses, and claim strengths, forming bonds that we call friendship. The patient breathes easier, smiles a little, and sees signs of hope.

That volunteer, also a cancer survivor, has experienced the recovery and rehabilitation of cancer and brief but intensive training—to understand the disease and its impact on patients and their families, to reflect on the personal dimensions of the cancer experience, to work in harmony with the team of caregivers, and above all to listen. The CanCare volunteer works as a member of a community of concern, one that insists that healing calls for partnership.

Visitors are assigned to contact persons with similar illness and similar situations, so the linkage is convenient and the shared energy flows both ways. Visitors meet their counterparts at home, in the hospital, at the work-place, or wherever confidential face-to-face visits can be arranged. Volunteers are nurtured for this work by comrade-ship with one another, personal attention from the staff, and education about health issues and resources. Celebrations bring together these valiant characters who support one another in this ministry and who are linked by dynamic prayer.

The CanCare volunteer serves with a lively community of concern for living cancer survivors. The emphasis is on heal-ing, hope, encouragement, joy, and quality of life. Motivated by varied religious commitments, CanCare's ministry reaches out to all persons with cancer who need these gifts. The sys-tem is supported by individuals, congregations, corporations, foundations. The Friends of CanCare (an auxiliary group) rally public interest and financial support for the committed visionary staff and the vigorous Board of Directors.

This complex network has become more than an efficient organization; it is a spiritual force. The healthy express grat-itude to God for their good health. Both those who are help-ing and those who are receiving help find new strength in working together. Together, they experience the divine heal-ing power they both need.

Nancy N. Tucker